# Educational Leadership in the Age of Greed

# A Requiem for *for* Res Publica

by

*Fenwick W.* **English**

**NCPEA Publications**

**National Council of Professors of Educational Administration**
**Ypsilanti, Michigan**

Published by NCPEA Publications
The publications of the National Council of Professors of Educational Administration (NCPEA)
http://www.ncpeapublications.org

Copyright © 2014 by Fenwick W. English and the National Council of Professors of Educational Administration

*All rights reserved.* No part of this book may be reproduced in any form or by any electronic or mechanical means, including information storage and retrieval systems, without written permission from the publisher, except by a reviewer who may quote passages in a review.

Printed in United States of America
*Library of Congress Cataloging-in-Publication Data*

English, Fenwick W.

Educational leadership in the age of greed

ISBN 978-1-4675-6538-7 (pbk)

How to order this book:

NCPEA Press, a book publisher for NCPEA Publications offers *Educational Leadership in the Age of Greed* as a Print-on-Demand hard copy and as an eBook at: www.ncpeapublication.org Books are prepared in Perfect Bound binding and delivery is 3-5 business days. eBooks are available upon ordering and delivered electronically in minutes to one's computer.

*Educational Leadership in the Age of Greed* is authored by Fenwick W. English, on the occasion of receiving the 2013 Living Legend Award from the National Council of Professors of Educational Administration. While this publication has been peer reviewed and accepted as a significant contribution to the preparation and practice of educational administration, the views expressed by Dr. English are not necessarily the official policy of the NCPEA, its Executive Board, Executive Director or the general membership.

| | |
|---|---|
| NCPEA Executive Director | James E. Berry |
| Publications Director and Production Editor | Theodore B. Creighton |
| NCPEA Publications Associate Director and Technical Editor | Brad E. Bizzell |
| Cover Design | Kyle Shorts |

# THIS BOOK POINTS THE SPEAR OF TRUTH TO TODAY'S CHALLENGES
*Front Piece*

*Autumn Cyprés*

This work points the spear of truth at the neoliberal antidote to the social challenges inside today's school systems and leadership preparation programs in an authentic democracy English deftly provides examples of benchmark events where the for profit approach to educational reform has injured or erased from American memory the purpose of school in an authentic democracy. He provides an easy-to-understand perspective that helps educators and those interested in education see beyond daily skill sets and challenges of school leadership. This result is a stunning gift because all too often we don't stop to think about how schools, society, and school leaders are enmeshed. English not only reveals the cause of modern constraints on schools, he offers a solution to improving the status quo. This journey leaves the reader simultaneously outraged and energized to contribute to the course corrections of how schools and the purpose of education are understood and currently supported.

Autumn Cyprés, Professor and Chair, Dept. of Ed. Leadership Virginia Commonwealth University

# FOREWORD
*Pièce de Résistance*

*Rosemary Papa*

How we think about our field is as important as what we feel is the freedom to express the democratic ideals and values expressed through our research and scholarship. There have been historic shifts in our thinking since our founding as the quote below illustrates.

> *During the past ten years a new "school" has developed within the profession of educational administration. Made up principally of youngish—theoreticians and research workers rather than practitioners or others whose chief work has been "in the field"—this new school has broken sharply with the past. Its parentage lies in scientific management, an offshoot of industrial engineering, peopled by professionals called "management consultants," who speak a language of their own. Hence this new school is a branch off the business tree, rather than a connecting link with "classical" school administration. Administrative Behavior in Education, edited by* Roald Campbell & Gregg Russell, first published 1957 *is the first comprehensive presentation of the views of this new school, which has received its developmental impetus from the annual sessions of the National Conference of Professors of Educational Administration and the beneficence of the W. K. Kellogg Foundation....*Vincent, W. (1959).

Clarion calls, that is a clear call for *résistance,* have changed in their number and appearance especially, in the last 30 to 50 years, as the movement from print to digital has exponentially shifted the spread of information, not knowledge, by the addition of global voices swept and pooled in the collective surrender to the business world behemoth. The quote above signified a fundamental shift in our field that occurred in the mid 1950's, and is one which we can document from NCPEA thinkers of that era. This quote also takes note of the historical bifurcation of NCPEA and UCEA.

In Dr. Fenwick English's Living Legend speech, *Educational Leadership in the Age of Greed: A Requiem for Res Publica*, he again sounds the clarion trumpet: a cry to rectify the potential demise of public education. It is in public education which was strongest during the mid-20th century that now crumbles from the decay of over-reliance on the *business tree* as noted above and today is called the neoliberal agenda.

Others too have raised that clarion call and for a time were heard. A most notable example was that of T.B. Greenfield (1975) who wrote, "Academicians who assume that social-scientific secrets can explain how organizations work or how policy should be made, indulge at best in premature hope and at worst in a delusion (p. 71)." Today, the digital era and global reality of world-wide inter-related economic forces have raised a cacophony of competing values with consequences that better some and hurt others. This is the schism of the *haves and have nots.*

When our scholarship is pure, voices can be heard. Fenwick English calls on us to face the reform-corruption found in the impact of the for-profit movement in public schooling. Can educational leadership scholars heed this call? We are today often marginalized. External voices that say we are not to be trusted. That we are corrupted and therefore should not be heard as we only represent our interests! That we have failed the field in our scholarship and research, therefore, for example, fully online programs for-profit companies must be accredited (Papa, 2011)! These voices believe we must be fixed and the fix is to open the doors to the business world so as for-profits can make money off the education field and the pseudo academic foundations can sell their products, all profiteering from their saying they have the correct reform to pursue.

The only way this era of reform is seen as viable and even remedying opportunities for profitability is because the war has been waged on public schooling for just over 30 years. Now, public universities and education professors are the last group to assault. The battles in pre-K-12 have thus far been lost.

Were we as a field possibly too silent in our scholarship over the last 30 years to defend public education? Were some, seeking self-fame, too eager to agree with these social and political forces of the day and in their haste compromised and dug the public education grave? As professional organizations joined the political band wagon of neoliberalism, e.g., the National Policy Board in Education Administration, some perceived that the *players* in this group diminished and sabotaged the voice of NCPEA as not the true voice of the field while heralding the unwarranted attacks on public schools, teachers, and administrators.

Dr. English through the NCPEA voice reminds us in his Living Legend speech/book there is much more to do: much more that we must do. One step NCPEA took eleven years ago was the initiation of the Living Legend Award, begun in 1999. NCPEA created this award as an intended posture to create *clarion callers* for the field of educational administration.

Briefly, the NCPEA criterion for the Living Legend Award is: living a life that inspires others, exemplary service to NCPEA, a model of genuine care, ethics, and professionalism in service to education dedicated to research, teaching and service to the profession, and, is a significant contributor to the field of educational administration. The list of previous NCPEA *clarion callers* who have been honored with the Living Legend Award are:

2013 Fenwick W. English
2012 James M. Smith
2011 Sandy Harris and I. Philip Young
2010 Lloyd DuVall
2009 Theodore Creighton
2008 Marilyn Grady
2007 Michael Martin
2006 Louis Wildman
2005 Clarence Fitch
2004 Robert Beach
2003 Rosemary Papa
2002 Martha McCarthy
2001 Chuck Achilles Deceased
2000 Jack Culbertson Deceased
1999 John Hoyle Deceased

Dr. English epitomizes the award of living a life of inspiration and profound service to the educational administration field. His book, *Educational Leadership in the Age of Greed: A Requiem for Res Publica,* bequeaths to our field a cry for action which gives testimony to the neoliberal business tree model he finds as an educational leader so destructive.. He writes of the regressive policy reforms constructed from greed that have corrupted public education.

Dr. English writes of the self-serving platform, the loss of civic humanism, and the erosion of the ethic of public service that accentuates larger social inequality in the U.S., as well the increase in the education achievement gap. On the wide shoulders of Pierre Bourdieu, Henry Giroux and many others he makes his case for social justice to be found in the societal need to maintain public space, that is by the public, for the public and which is accountable to the public.

Dr. English emphasizes the neoliberal argument that private property and pursuits promoting individual choices are not values that protect the common good. Private enterprise can survive without a value to the common good for their existence endures as long as their profitability grows. He cites several companies, e.g., Apple, Amazon, Starbucks, etc., that hide money out of the U.S. This is the new global business plan: ignore and have little responsibility to the country that helped create them (educated workforce, tax breaks to establish corporation, federal, state, and country abeyances, etc.) and enabled them to flourish.

These companies have lobbied to become via reform initiatives in pursuit of profit a growing slice of the educational pie, all the while also lobbying for less taxes and have further corporate reductions while stashing billions of dollars in taxable income off shore. He reminds us that while tax dodging in what they and other corporations are doing is not illegal, the values question does arise: "Is this fair and is this the right way to act? Who is benefitting? And, who is being harmed?

Dr. English's words are meant to rankle us to take action. In the past he has faced being ostracized by a few in the educational administration profession for *just not going along in the denunciation to make money or gain perceived self-importance and power.* His writing, *The Ten Most Wanted Enemies of American Public Education's School Leadership* (2010) sparked a few of the go-alongs to ask him to apologize for saying truths which exposed some of the profiteers-charlatans and asked to rewrite ideas to make them more Rightest.

He expands on this earlier writing by adding a table of those who advocate neoliberalism and their positions. Additionally, he and his graduate student Zan Crowder, note in the Appendix the Eli Broad, l 'enfant terrible, class of graduates schooled on anti-education preparation, anti-union busting, and the business profitability philosophy.

Dr. English believes we, the educational leaders, must through the force of our voices, scholarship, teaching, service and research, identify the neoliberal agendas and self-interests found in their proposals for reform and call them out. He asks us to be brave and vigorously describe the horrific effects of what I term anti-educationists reform prophets. His book epitomizes the NCPEA Living Legend award in that it is meant to inspire us to action; it calls on us to defend the defenseless, and is most significant in its bravery to call out those in pursuit of changing public education based on the doctrine of greed. The clarion calls. The trumpet sounds. Dr. English's *pièce de résistance* invites us to join the resistance.

# Contents

| | | |
|---|---|---|
| *Front Piece* | **The Spear of Truth to Today's Challenges**<br>*Autumn Cyprés* | iii |
| *Foreword* | **Pièce de Résistance**<br>*Rosemary Papa* | iv |
| **Section 1** | **Introduction** | 1 |
| **Section 2** | **The Thirty Year Neoliberal Assault on Public Education**<br>*2.1 Milton Friedman: Portrait of a Weberian "Switchman"* | 3 |
| **Section 3:** | **The Rise of Regressive Policy Passed off as Educational Reform**<br>*3.1 The Major Steps of the Neoliberal Assault on Public Education*<br>*3.2 The Nature of the Education Industry and Rise of the EMO*<br>*3.3 The For-Profit Mindset and its Danger to the Individual*<br>*3.4 Beware of Neoliberal Research: A Legacy of Racism, Elitism, and Half Truths* | 6 |
| **Section 4** | **De-Constructing the Claims of a L'Enfant Terrible: Eli Broad and His Neoliberal Educational Crusade** | 23 |
| **Section 5** | **The Installation of Greed as a Raison d'etre of Leadership and the Resulting Culture of Corruption**<br>*5.1 Stiglitz' Explanation for the Existence of a Culture of Corruption as the Norm*<br>*5.2 Lack of Transparency and Keeping Your Customers or Regulators Ignorant in Order to Take Advantage, Mislead, Deceive, or Bilk Them*<br>*5.3 Finding Loopholes and Cutting Corners to Push Profits*<br>*5.4 Colluding with Competitors to Keep Prices High and Avoid Free Market Economies*<br>*5.5 Stealing Trade Secrets from Competitors*<br>*5.6 The Violation of the Public Benchmarks of Justice and Fairness* | 30 |
| **Section 6** | **The Culture of Corruption Comes to Education**<br>*6.1 The Crooked Future is Already Here Big Time: The Case for For-Profit Higher Education*<br>*6.2 "Kick Ass" Management and the Proliferation of the Cheating Scandals*<br>    *A. Michelle Rhee and the Washington, D.C. "Your fired" Neoliberal Playbook*<br>    *B. Lorenzo Garcia: The El Paso Miracle Man Becomes The First School Superintendent Sent to the Slammer for Fake Test Score Gains*<br>    *C. Beverly Hall, Maven of Bonus Pay and the Pervasive Culture of Cheating in Atlanta*<br>    *D. The School/Society Nexus and the Achievement Gap* | 37 |

| | | |
|---|---|---|
| *Section 7* | **The Age of Greed and the Iron Cage of Schooling** | **49** |
| *Section 8* | **Conclusions: A Strategy for "Regressionsverbot"** | **51** |
| *Section 9* | **Pursuing Pushback to Corporate Reform** | **57** |
| *Epilogue* | Reclaiming Public Education<br>*Carol A. Mullen* | 60 |
| ***About the Author and Contributors*** | | **78** |
| *Appendix A* | **Appendix A**- A Record of the Career Trajectories of the Broad Superintendent's Academy Graduates 2004-2011 by Zan Crowder | 80 |
| *Index* | | **94** |

# INTRODUCTION

We are living through the time when public education as we have known it in America will be forever transformed unless concerted action is undertaken to reverse the trends described in this book. If nothing is done to stop these trends there will be no going back. The great American dream for a common school which would serve all the children of all the people under the umbrella of fostering the common good will vanish forever.

These were the schools in which I was educated and my mother and father worked as public school teachers. They were the schools my own children and grand children enjoyed. Our grand children may be the last generation to experience the fruits of Horace Mann's hard fought legacy when he said toward the end of his struggle for public education, "Be ashamed to die until you have won some victory for humanity" (Messerli, 1971, p. 549.) It is Mann's admonition that has prompted this book as my *NCPEA Living Legend Award* speech for 2013.

The public schools in America have been the contested social space where legitimacy, influence, and societal power were decided. Even from the beginning they were far from perfect and harmonious places (Katz, 1973; Tyack, 1974; Labaree, 1988; Ravitch, 2000). They have been the nation's idealistic and ideological battlegrounds when the interests of the common community to live up to the promise that they would serve as the socio-economic ladder to a better life for all children were pitted against the interests of the few who wanted them to preserve their social and economic position of dominance (Watkins, 2012).

What we are witnessing is what Pierre Bourdieu (1999a) has called "the destruction of the idea of public service" (p. 182) in which so-called "reformers" and their legislative friends and accomplices will have turned educational leadership into corporate, for profit, run by the numbers *managerialism* in which "teaching becomes a technology that can be observed, deconstructed, analyzed, costed, measured and packaged" (Gunter, 1997, p. viii) in-other-words *commodified*.

This near thirty year transformation has been ruthlessly pursued with huge sums of money spent on a broad front assault beginning with the abandonment of the idea of *res publica*, education as a public service for the public, that is, *for all* (Boyle & Burns, 2012). These agents and agencies:

> *...suggest that since inequalities are unavoidable, the struggle against them is ineffective (which does not keep them from blaming the system for discouraging the best people) and, in any case, can only be undertaken to the detriment of freedom; by associating efficiency and modernity with private enterprise, and archaism and inefficiency with the public sector, they seek to substitute the relationship with the customer, supposedly more egalitarian and more effective, for the relation to the user; finally, they identify 'modernization' with the transfer into the private sector of the public services with the most profit potential and with eliminating or bringing into line subordinate staff in the public services, held responsible for every inefficiency and every 'rigidity'* (Bourdieu, 1999b, p. 182).

The agenda being advanced on a global basis has a name (Mullen, Samier, Brindley, English & Carr, 2012). It is called *neoliberalism* and it has been defined by Harvey (2005) as "a theory of political economic practices that proposes that human well-being can best be advanced by liberating individual entrepreneurial freedoms and skills within an institutional framework characterized by strong private property rights, free markets, and free trade" (p. 2).

Neoliberalism is an ideology, that is a, "belief system shared by the members of a collectivity" (Parsons, 1951, p. 331). It is that belief system that is being imposed on education and which is the subject of critique in this book along the lines of Merton's (1968) distinction between a lie and an untruth:

> *Awareness of ideological thought comes when an adversary's assertions are regarded as untrue by their determination by his life-situation. Since it is not assumed that these distortions are deliberate, the ideology differs from the lie. Indeed, the distinction between the two is essential in as much as it emphasizes the unwitting nature of ideological statements* (p. 546).

According to Kumar (2012) the neoliberal agenda has two dimensions.

> *(1) while it draws education into the marketplace and transforms it into a commodity that can be traded and thus make contribution to expansion of capital, (2) it also transforms the character (content) of education, which not only gets reduced to skill development and therefore creates an army of labor force required by capital at this particular historical moment, but also ensures that criticality remains a distant agenda of education* (p. 7).

It will be the purpose of this book to describe the neoliberal assault on the idea of the common school which first requires an erasure of the belief in such an idea, and secondly the destruction of the institutions and the means by which leaders are prepared to lead them in the pursuit of that belief.

In short, the neoliberal assault is about replacing equality as manifested in an agenda of social justice, with inequality as an agenda of enshrining privilege in the mantle of efficiency. It is the perpetuation of Frederick Taylor's scientific management morphed into a contemporary political ideology, and of Max Weber's (1930) notion of the "iron cage" replete with the language of managerial perfection possible only in a machine bureaucracy where the answer to nearly all problems is "when in doubt control" (Mintzberg, 1983, p. 180).

As we shall see the imposition of the "iron cage" is accompanied by a form of extreme routinization which enables control to be established and maintained. It is the type of control which requires elaborate, pervasive and ruthless conformity and standardization accompanied by a *for profit* mindset which is so destructive to the ethos of public service, responsibility and accountability.

# THE THIRTY-YEAR NEOLIBERAL ASSAULT ON PUBLIC EDUCATION

Public education has always had its critics (Scott & Hill, 1954). Despite such criticism over time Americans have displayed a remarkable confidence in the public schools, so much so that public education has been considered a form of civil religion (Bankston & Caldas, 2009). But something happened beginning over thirty years ago which has undermined that confidence. To understand that development it is useful to employ Max Weber's notion of how cultural change occurs with the railroad metaphor of "the switchmen" (Schroeder, 1992).

Weber (1946) believed that a new model or world view was established by a charismatic individual who broke the mold by laying new tracks. Weber's metaphor was that of the railroad "switchman". Ideas were new intellectual/conceptual rails. However he also observed that, "Not ideas, but material and ideal interests, directly govern men's conduct" (p.280). We shall see this rather clearly in the neoliberal attack on public education and the advancement of the material interests of its supporters as they see the profits to be made for its pursuit in wresting a public service into a private space, a process called *commodification*.

## Milton Friedman: Portrait of a Weberian "Switchman"

Milton Friedman's 1962 publication of *Capitalism and Freedom* marks the rise of the charismatic prophet described by Max Weber who lays down a new set of rails for subsequent trains to follow. Madrick (2011) says of him, "Friedman's ingenuity, persistence, and articulateness were the sources of his attractiveness. In the 1970s, there was no other intellectual force comparable to him on America's right" (p. 28). And there is little doubt that Milton Friedman *was* charismatic.

Paul Krugman (2007), a professional economist at Princeton University, summarized Friedman's career saying that "…Milton Friedman was a very great man indeed—a man of intellectual courage who was one of the most important economic thinkers of all time, and possible the most brilliant communicator of economic ideas to the general public that ever lived" (p. 30).

Friedman was a passionate voice for free markets. He argued that government depended on centralized authority which posed a threat to individual freedom. He conceded that "government is necessary to preserve our freedom" because "it is an instrument through which we can exercise our freedom" (1962, p. 2). Yet even as government provided some guarantee of personal liberty, there was always danger that over time the power in government would lead to corruption because "it will both attract and form men of a different stamp" (p. 2).

The solution to this dilemma regarding government was to limit its scope and to disperse its power because, "Government can never duplicate the variety and diversity of individual action" (p. 4). The solution, according to Friedman, was "competitive capitalism" and he defined it as "the organization of the bulk of economic activity through private enterprise operating in a free market—as a system of economic freedom and a necessary condition for political freedom" (p. 4).

Friedman devoted considerable attention to the role of government in education. He found current practices objectionable for the preparation and licensing of teachers arguing that, "The efficient way to get control over the number in a profession is therefore to get control of entry into professional schools" (p. 151). He found the practice of using standard salary schedules for teachers objectionable because "poor teachers are grossly overpaid and good teachers grossly underpaid" (p.95). He was opposed to any practice that arose which led to monopoly because this condition resulted in "a limitation on voluntary exchange through a reduction in the alternatives available to individuals" (p. 120). When a monopoly exists the individual has no choice to alter the terms of exchange and the monopolist has a reduced social responsibility.

Finally Friedman argued for governments to provide parents with vouchers "redeemable for a specified maximum sum per child per year if spent on 'approved' educational services…The educational services could be rendered by private enterprises operated for profit, or by non-profit institutions" (p. 89).

It is clear where Friedman placed his emphasis in *Capitalism and Freedom*. It was on individual choice and not on societal responsibilities to individuals. His argument was that economic freedom equated to political freedom and that "the role of the market, as already noted, is that it permits unanimity without conformity; that it is a system of effectively proportional representation" (p. 23).

This position is the epitome of the neoliberal/libertarian platform. The role of the state is to ensure individual liberty and not be concerned with larger societal issues such as poverty, health care, social security and education. The responsibility of the state is not to ensure that all children have a quality education. It is rather to ensure that individuals have choices to obtain for themselves a quality education.

Friedman, as well as his neoliberal acolytes, ignored the fact that there is no level playing field for individuals or groups in the larger society and that, "…the introduction of choice into public services invariable slants provision towards the better placed and better educated members of the society" (Barry, 2005, p. 137). Choice thus increases the gap between the haves and have nots and does not reduce inequality. Neoliberals dismiss such concerns by saying that the free market will take care of that. They then point out that if some children receive a poor education within a free market then it was the result of poor decisions on the part of those making their educational choices.

This perspective enables neoliberals to avoid accepting any responsibility of the state to provide good schools for all children. It is thus an acceptance that there will almost always be poor schools around, but that is not the responsibility of the state to be concerned about them. The responsibility of the state is to create more choices for consumers, to deregulate all aspects of schooling, and to break the so-called "harmful monopoly" of the current educational system (see Klein, 2011).

It also keeps the costs of state education low and those that normally pay the most in taxes, which would be the more privileged individuals in a society, from paying more for such education for the poor. This position prompted Pierre Bourdieu (1998) to echo what Max Weber said that the "dominant groups always need a 'theodicy of their own privilege,' or more precisely, a sociodicy, in other words a theoretical justification of the fact that they are privileged" (p. 43).

Further, Bourdieu (1998) called this neoliberal tenet, "a very smart and very modern repackaging of the oldest ideas of the oldest capitalists" (p. 34) acknowledging simultaneously that while neoliberalism appealed to the notions of progress, reason and science what that really meant was "the return to a kind of radical capitalism, with no other law than that of maximum profit, an unfettered capitalism without any disguise, but rationalized, pushed to the limit of its economic efficacy…"(p. 35).

Friedman also drew criticism of other academic economists. Paul Krugman (2007) said of him, "While Friedman's theoretical work is universally admired by professional economists, there's much more ambivalence about his policy pronouncements and especially his popularizing. And it must be said that there were some serious questions about his intellectual honesty when he was speaking to the mass public (p. 27).

Madrick (2011) offered a similar synopsis of Friedman's work when he said that, "He [Friedman] insisted he was not ideological, and adamantly claimed he based his theories on facts. In this, he exaggerated greatly…His academic research, sometimes usefully provocative, was controversial and usually not adequate to justify his many claims" (p.27).

Stephen A. Marglin (2009), a professor of economics at Harvard, indicates that "economics is a two faced discipline. It claims to be a science, describing the world without preconception or value judgment" but "the reality is that descriptive economics has been shaped by a framework of assumptions geared more to its normative message than to its pretensions" (p. B10). Marglin then explained:

*The self-interested individual—who rationally calculates how to achieve ever more consumption, whose conception of community is limited to the nation-state—is a myth, not exactly false but a half-truth at best. That framework is essential to the normative side of an economics that proclaims the virtues of markets and is maintained even when it gets in the way of understanding how the economy really works (p. B10).*

Despite the limitations of Friedman's popular works, his followers saw great opportunities to implement his ideas along the tracks he laid. Many were already predisposed to follow them and there was no shortage of money from conservative individuals and foundations to implement them. But it was Friedman as the conceptual "switchman" that "provided the intellectual map for a reversal of the progressive evolution of the nation" (Madrick, 2011, p. 27).

Friedman's lingering ghost over current political debates is still felt. For example, Stephen Moore (2013), a member of the *Wall Street Journal's* editorial board, claims that the Nobel winning economist viewed legal and illegal immigration as a good thing. Why? Because Friedman indicated that illegal immigrants, "don't qualify for welfare and social security" (p.A13). Thus, illegal immigrants contribute to the economy the fruits of their labors, but they can't qualify for taxpayer support for other social support services. This anecdote about Friedman also indicates the absolutely coldly calculated equations of the neoliberals and their ideology towards those less fortunate.

# THE RISE OF REGRESSIVE POLICY PASSED OFF AS EDUCATIONAL REFORM

Calling neoliberalism a "fatalistic doctrine" because it presents itself as inevitability wrapped in common sense, Bourdieu (1998) wrote that it "gives itself the air of a message of liberation, through a whole series of lexical tricks around the idea of freedom, liberation, deregulation, etc., a whole series of euphemisms or ambiguous uses of words—'reform,' for example—designed to present a restoration as a revolution, in a logic which is that of all conservative revolutions" (p. 50).

The bridge from Milton Friedman's neoliberal role of Weberian "switchman" to a translation into policy and ultimately practice takes four major temporal/conceptual steps. These are culled from the literature. They are shown in Figure 1 below:

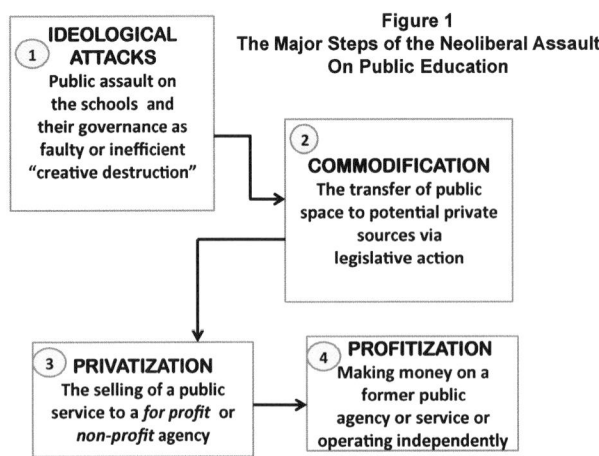

Recasting the image of the public schools has taken a concerted and well funded assault over many decades, but the result has been the loss of faith in the role of public education to the point where the chief synonym for them is "failed" (Emery & Ohanian, 2004).

> *Public schools once occupied a distinct place in the culture of American democracy. The American common school ideal (if not always in reality) was democratic in ambition and purpose. It was part of the social fabric, yet set apart from mass culture, and as such was charged with the task of enabling sand empowering successive generations to take their place as citizens in a complex, democratic society* (Molnar, 2005, p. 16).

Funded by conservative foundations and channeling millions of dollars into this effort, "puts [all] the intellectual resources that money can mobilize in the service of economic interests (as with the 'think tanks' where hired thinkers and mercenary researchers are brought together with journalists and public relations experts" (Bourdieu, 2001, p.77) who churn out position papers, reports, op-ed pieces, and more often than not shoddy research which is sent straight to newspapers and rarely vetted at rigorous professional research conferences.

Right wing philanthropic organizations are organized for the long haul and they have worked hard to build institutional infrastructure (Krehely, House & Kernan, 2004; Henninger, 2012). "The Right especially targets funding to organizations that aggressively lobby in state legislatures and Congress, and that engage effectively in media campaigns, thus ensuring that Rightest ideas are enacted into law with public support" (Kumashiro, 2008, p. 11).

**The Major Steps of the Neoliberal Assault on Public Education**

*Step 1: Ideological Attacks and the Rise of the Neoliberal Think Tanks*

In the early 1970s two young conservative legislative aides, Ed Feulner and Phil Crane, established the Heritage Foundation, affectionately known by neoliberals and their supporters as "the Beast" (Feulner & Needham, 2010). Generously funded by beer baron Joseph Coors and the Sarah Mellon Scaife Foundation, it was dedicated to the creation of a resurgent repository of conservative ideas of how to transform government and other public services (Hacker & Pierson, 2010, p.123).

According to an interview of Ed Feulner at the time of his retirement in 2012, Heritage always had a primary focus that was clear from the beginning. He told *The Wall Street Journal*, "We defined our audience specifically. It is Congress and congressional staff. That's why we we're here on Capitol Hill. That's our target" (Henninger, 2012, p. A15.)

It's first major accomplishment was to deliver a 1,093 report to the newly installed Reagan administration in 1980 on a broad array of policy initiatives which over the next four decades became the cornerstone of neoliberal positions such as, "welfare reform, partial privatization of Social Security, market-based health-care reform, tuition tax credits, education vouchers, inner-city enterprise zones, free trade, missile defense and much more" (Edwards, 2013, p. A13).

Later in its operations Heritage writers focused on writing papers they called "backgrounders" limited to only 10 to 15 pages. The first two-thirds of a "backgrounder" were only the facts. Heritage's conservative perspective was saved until the last part and identified as its policy on the topic (Henninger, 2012).

Heritage also has taken steps to establish an advocacy organization called *Heritage Action for America* which would have the ability to pressure legislators:

> *There are 110 congressional districts in America with over 1,500 Heritage supporters apiece. Two-thirds of the congressional districts in this country have over 1,000 Heritage members each. Now they will have an advocacy organization that can press Congress on their behalf...Heritage Action for America will guarantee that when a wavering congressman thinks of voting for higher taxes, increased regulation, or a weaker national defense, television ads in his home district will remind him that a vote for bigger government is a vote for less freedom* (p. A19).

Heritage is considered the premier type of right wing think tank which others emulated such as the American Enterprise Institute of Public Policy; the Cato Institute; Center for

Education Reform; and the Hoover Institution at Stanford. State level conservative think tanks include the Evergreen Freedom Foundation in Olympia, Washington; Heartland Institute in Chicago, Independence Institute in Golden, Colorado, the Manhattan Institute in New York City, the Reason Foundation in Los Angeles (Kumarshiro, 2008, p. 14) and the Thomas B. Fordham Institute in Dayton, Ohio (Maxwell, 2006). A recent neoliberal newcomer is the George W. Bush Institute of Dallas, Texas.

The neoliberal think tanks are bankrolled by big money from far right donors that include what is called the four "Big Sister" foundations which are the Lynde and Harry Bradley Foundation which have backed initiatives to end affirmative action and welfare and are sponsors of school voucher programs and privatization as well as backers of the George W. Bush Institute; the John M. Olin Foundation (which has subsequently gone out of business); the Scaife Family Foundation (Mellon Bank) and the H. Smith Richardson Foundation. These foundations have supported the American Enterprise Institute, Heritage and the Hoover Institution to name a few. In addition the Walton Family Foundation of Arkansas "Is the most influential foundation in promoting school vouchers and has financed nearly every ballot initiative for vouchers since 1993" (Kumashiro, 2008, p. 13) and the DeVos Foundation (think AmWay) also is a strong supporter of school vouchers. The Koch brothers, Charles and David, owners of Koch Industries with estimated total revenue of $100 billion, helped found the Cato Institute and the Libertarian Party. They are long time backers of right wing causes (Luskin, 2011, p. A15).

Other attack groups promoting the neoliberal agenda are the creation of specific advocacy groups beyond the more academic and policy type of institutions such as AEI or Heritage. Among them is StudentsFirst, an advocacy and lobbying group established by Michelle Rhee, the controversial former chancellor of the Washington, D.C. public schools and the darling of the neoliberal educational ideologues (Fields, 2008).

Rhee advocates government sponsored vouchers so students could attend private schools, "rating principals based on student performance and getting rid of teacher tenure" (Banchero, 2011b, p. A7). Rhee's organization gave $250,000 to certain candidates in the hotly contested school board race in Los Angeles who espoused the type of ideological change she pushed as former Chancellor of the Washington, D.C. Public Schools (Strauss, 2013). It has been reported that StudentsFirst received a gift of $50 million from Rupert Murdoch, the conservative owner of *The Wall Street Journal* which runs frequent articles and opinion pieces from the conservative think tanks in that national newspaper (Sawchuk, 2012, pp 1, 16, 18).

Harvey (2005) uses the term "creative destruction, (p. 3) to describe how neoliberals go about their ideological attacks on "traditional forms of state sovereignty" right down to "habits of the heart" (p. 3). In this important first step shown in Figure 1 Rupert Murdoch's op-ed pages of the *Wall Street Journal* have become "…the country's most influential newspaper pages—regularly supply more support and valuable ideas to the conservative establishment than any other paper or magazine" (Wolff, 2008, p. 257). "An odd and fundamental truth about the *WSJ* is that it is a profoundly conservative newspaper—irascibly and militantly conservative" (Wolff, 2010, p. 257).

The *WSJ* has been the major attack dog of the neoliberal assault on public education over the years. It has run op-ed pieces by famous and infamous neoliberals, many of whom work for and are supported by the neoliberal think tanks who churn out a form of social

Darwinistic and racist pieces of writing to support vouchers, charter schools and advocate making legislative war on teacher unions and putting an end to teacher tenure.

For example, Jason Riley (2011), a member of the *Wall Street Journal's* editorial board wrote, "Teacher unions agitate for laws and regulations that ban means-tested voucher programs or cap the number of charter schools that can open in a state. To protect jobs for their members, they fight to keep the worst instructors from being fired and the worst schools from closing" (p. A13). The fact that, where objectively measured, the record of charter schools to improve student achievement is the same or worse *The Wall Street Journal* chooses to ignore (see Miron & Nelson, 2002

Another report on charter schools was issued by the Economic Policy Institute which said, "…the claims made by many charter school supporters that charter schools would elicit sizable learning improvements, on average, because charter schools would be free of school bureaucracies and union contracts, has proven groundless. It seems that bureaucracy and union contracts have not been the cause of disadvantaged students' low performance, at least on average" (Carnoy, Jacobsen, Mishel & Rothstein (2005, pp. 125-6). The National Education Policy Center located at the University of Colorado at Boulder has issued numerous reviews of charter school research over the years that also disputes the claims made by its supporters. These also fail to make the editorial pages of *The Wall Street Journal*.

Here are some examples of the tight connection between prominent neoliberal advocates, many on the payrolls of neoliberal foundations and institutes or who have established their neoliberal agencies, who have appeared on the op-ed pages of *WSJ* over the years.

**Charles Murray** (2005) of the American Enterprise Institute wrote a caustic op-ed piece after Hurricane Katrina when he spoke of a permanent underclass (viz. African American) population that, "Unemployment in the underclass is not caused by lack of jobs or of job skills, but by the inability to get up every morning and go to work…You name it, we've tried it. It doesn't work with the underclass" (p. A18).

**Jeb Bush** (2006) former Republican governor of Florida wrote about the five rules for school reform which was from a lecture he gave at Stanford University's Hoover Institution in which he said, "Our choice programs include corporate tax credit scholarships for use at private schools so low-income parents have the same options that wealthier families have…" (p. A19.)

**Louis Gerstner, Jr.**, (2008) former CEO of IBM wrote that one way to improve education was to "abolish all local school districts save 70 (50 states; 20 largest cities" and to "measure student and teacher performance on a systematic basis, supported by tests and assessments" (p. A23).

**Eli Broad** (Riley, 2009) billionaire neoliberal who has established his own academy to prepare school superintendents says, "…it is time to get rid of education schools—'they're the lowest ranking students at a university'" (p. A11).

**Eric Hanushek** (2010) of the Hoover Institution at Stanford singled out teacher unions because they protect poor teachers and did not represent "the vast numbers of highly effective teachers" (p. A-17).

**Chester E. Finn, Jr.** (2010) a fellow at Stanford's Hoover Institute and President of the Thomas E. Fordham Institute (supported by the Broad Foundation), reviewed the latest

PISA test scores and seeing that China's Shanghai's outscored 15 year olds in 65 countries claimed that this amounted to "a sputnik moment for U.S. education" (p. A21). Asking a rhetorical question, "Will this news be the wakeup call that America needs to get serious about educational achievement?" Finn repeats the familiar neoliberal solutions.

**Joel Klein** (2010) former New York City School Chancellor and now and Executive Vice President of News Corporation owned by Rupert Murdoch says that, "…traditional proposals for improving education—more money, better curriculum, smaller classes, etc.---aren't going to get the job done…we also increased choices for families by replacing almost 100 failing schools with about 500 new, small schools designed with community and charter management groups" (p. A13)

**Rupert Murdoch** (2010) media mogul and owner of *The Wall Street Journal* argues that inner city schools are "failing our children" but works well for adults such as teachers who are protected by teachers' unions. Saying that "We have tougher standards on 'American Idol' than for schools, Mr. Murdoch indicates that there is "zero incentive for adapting new technologies that could help learning inside and outside the classroom" (p. A19). Mr. Murdoch then hires former NYC Chancellor Joel Klein to head a new division in News Corporation called Wireless Generation, which is aimed at installing digital technologies in classrooms (Martinez and Saul, 2010, p. A4). It is estimated that the total market Murdoch wants to expand into is worth about $500 billion per year (Adams & Vascellaro, 2010).

**Michelle Rhee** (2011), founder and CEO of StudentsFirst, an organization devoted to implementing neoliberal cures for public schools such as mayoral control of public schools (p. A-17).

**Jeb Bush** and **Joel Klein** (2011), a former Republican Governor of Florida and Mr. Klein, former chancellor of the New York City Schools and now an employee of News Corporation owned by Rupert Murdoch, argue for the Common Core Curriculum because "America's economic strength and standing in the world economy are directly linked to our ability to equip students with the knowledge and skills to succeed in the 21$^{st}$-century economy" (p. A13.

**Frederick Hess** (2012) of the AEI argued that the fear of "for profit education" was irrational and that "for-profits have a relentless, selfish imperative to seek out and adopt cost efficiencies," while the "nonprofits, by contrast, have little incentive to become 'early adopters' of cost-saving tools and techniques such as online instruction" (p.A-15).

**Rex Sinquefield** (Riley, 2012). Mr. Sinquefield is an index fund pioneer and a staunch conservative who has given money to Karl Rove and his Super PAC. Mr. Sinquefield has spent somewhere around $21 million on various causes some of which have gone to education reform and to the repeal of taxes, campaign spending limits, and to the perpetuation of free markets. "In 2014, Mr. Sinquefield is planning his most ambitious ballot initiative to date: abolishing teacher tenure in Missouri" (p. A13.)

The journal has also featured op-ed pieces promoting mayoral control of urban schools, a favorite neoliberal "cure" for urban school systems with low test scores or graduation rates (see Hechinger & Sataline, 2009).

*Table 1* is a brief partial summary of some of the broad based attacks on public schools, the governance structure, leadership preparation, teaching, teacher tenure, teacher unions, and the advocates for the changes specific neoliberals support. The neoliberal agenda amounts to an ideology, that is, "…ideology amounts to the totality of ideas, concepts, and representations which do not come under the heading of science" (Boudon, 1989, p. 18).

Table 1
*A Partial Summary of Neoliberal Positions and Their Major Advocates*

| **Neoliberal Position** | **Name of Advocate(s)** |
|---|---|
| Abolition of teacher tenure | Eli Broad, Michelle Rhee, Rex Sinquefield, Chester Finn |
| Abolition of collective bargaining for teacher unions or opposed to teacher unions | Frederick Hess, Eric Hanushek, Joel Klein |
| Abolition of licensing for teachers and educational leaders | Frederick Hess, Milton Friedman, Chester Finn |
| Abolition of school boards replaced with mayoral control of schools | Michael Bloomberg, Arne Duncan |
| Abolition of the free high school | Milton Friedman |
| Abolition of Schools of Education | Eli Broad, Chester Finn, |
| Installation of a standardized, national curriculum (the "Common Core") | Jeb Bush, Joel Klein, Louis Gerstner, Arne Duncan, Bill Gates |
| Advocacy of *for-profit* schools | Frederick Hess |
| Merit pay for teachers | Eli Broad, Louis Gerstner |
| Standardized testing as part of teacher evaluation | Louis Gerstner, Michelle Rhee |
| Abolition of local school districts | Louis Gerstner |
| Creation of Charter Schools to Replace Public Schools | Joel Klein, Michelle Rhee, Bill Gates, Arne Duncan |
| Advocacy of non-educators in leadership positions | Frederick Hess, Chester Finn Jr., Eli Broad |
| Advocacy of voucher plans to enable students to attend private and/or religious schools | Michelle Rhee, Jeb Bush, Chester Finn, John Walton |
| Avoid paying teachers for advanced graduate degrees | Michelle Rhee, Bill Gates |

*Step 2: Commodification of Public Space via Legislative Enactment*

Commodification refers to the reconceptualization of public space or assets and recasting them as commodities to be bought and sold. The sale of public space dedicated to the performance of a public service usually requires legislative enactment. It means that laws and policies must be changed to permit public education to be sliced and diced and sold, in whole or in parts. And there is a difference between schools being used for commercial activities and the actual schoolhouse being sold as an entity.

Molnar (2005) indicates that in 2002 the Council on Corporate and School Partnerships estimated that the schools received approximately $2.4 billion a year from commercial relationships with businesses that ranged from sponsoring certain programs to fund scholarships or exclusive agreements with vendors to sell soft drinks or confections in schools or even underwrite the costs of an electronic scoreboard for the football stadium displaying corporate logos.

The line is crossed from commercialism to commodification when the actual space is sold and the buyer can operate independently from the seller and perform a heretofore public service in a market determined by profit. This line becomes thin in practice. Take the case of Chris Whittle's 1980 venture in Channel One.

The exchange of space in a public school for Channel One went something like this. Whittle would "give" the school television sets and VCRs "free" in return for having all students watch the news each morning. Whittle then sold programming advertising for candy bars, cosmetics and clothing on the news program to a captive audience. At its height, Channel One was found in 350,000 classrooms reaching eight million students (Saltman, 2005, p.23.) Clearly this is an example of commodifying a formally public space into an owned for profit site which then operated independently of the seller. Later, Whittle came to understand that what really would be profitable was the actual running of whole schools. Thus, was born the Edison Project where a corporation would run for a profit dozens of schools in U.S. cities.

The problem with commodification is that "the introduction of market incentives and mechanisms can change people's attitudes and crowd out nonmarket values" (Sandel, 2012, p. 121). Henry Giroux (2004) summarized this shift as follows:

*Under neoliberal globalization, capital removes itself from any viable form of state regulation, power is uncoupled from matters of ethics and social responsibility, and market freedoms replace long-standing social contracts that once provided a safety net for the poor, the elderly, workers, and the middle class* (p. 59).

Perhaps no more striking example could be discerned than the case of Apple, Inc. that under the scrutiny of the United States Senate Permanent Subcommittee on Investigations revealed that at least $74 billion had been stashed abroad so that the company paid little or no corporate taxes in the last four years (Linebaugh, Lessin & Yadron, 2013). Some of Apple's foreign subsidiaries were little more than empty shills which employed no employees and were "stateless—exempt from taxes, record-keeping laws and the need for subsidiaries to even file tax returns anywhere in the world" (Schwartz, 2013, p.A-4).

Apple responded by saying that it paid corporate income taxes in the amount of $6 billion in 2012. Senator John McCain, the ranking Republican on the subcommittee, subsequently commented, "What they often leave out is the second part of the story, that Apple is one of the largest tax avoiders" (Linebaugh, Lessin & Yadron, 2013, p. A1.) For example, in 2011, one Irish based Apple subsidiary recorded sales in the amount of $22 billion but paid just $10 million in taxes, "That works out to a rate of about .05%" (Linebaugh, Lessin & Yadron, 2013, p. A2). A law professor at the University of Southern California, a former staff official at the Congressional Joint Committee on Taxation said, "There is a technical term economists like to use for behavior like this—unbelievable chutzpah" (Schwartz, 2013, p.A-4).

A *New York Times* editorial declared "American corporations now have an estimated $2 trillion stashed abroad" saying that "Rampant corporate tax avoidance may not be illegal, but that doesn't make it right or fair" (*New York Times*, 2013, p. 10). Giroux's (2004) warning that, "Neoliberalism empties the public treasury, privatizes formerly public services, limits the vocabulary and imagery available to recognize anti-democratic forms of power, and reinforces narrow models of individual agency" (p. 49) is thus prescient.

And Apple, Inc is not the only U.S., corporation involved in such practices. Senate hearings also examined Google, Amazon and Starbucks for tax avoidance while it was noted that General Electric paid no taxes at all in 2010.

The net effect is that:

*As corporate tax revenue has withered as a share of the economy and as a share of total revenue, Washington has leaned more heavily on individuals to pay for government. In 2012, personal income taxes and payroll taxes raised $1.9 trillion, compared with $242 billion raised from corporate taxes, a disparity that contributes to widening inequality and, in turn, to a slow economy and less social mobility. Congress's Joint Committee on Taxation estimates that fully taxing the profits sheltered abroad by American corporations would raise an additional $42 billion in revenue this year, enough to end more than half the spending cuts in the sequester* (New York Times, 2013, p. 10).

There are few checks on corporate power today. The same fear that Friedman (1962) had about government arriving at a monopoly also applies to multinational corporations. Friedman (1962) said then, "Exchange is truly voluntary only when nearly equivalent alternatives exist. Monopoly implies the absence of alternatives and thereby inhibits effective freedom of exchange" (p. 28).

The lack of freedom of exchange between even corporations and their shareholders is exemplified in the flap over executive pay. Recently, a majority of shareholders of the H.J. Heinz Company voted down a golden parachute of $55 million for retiring Chief Executive Officer William Johnson. It had no effect at all on the outcome prompting an official in the Institutional Shareholder Services to remark,"The question is, who is to be held accountable and what for?" (Monga, 2013, B4.)

*Step 3: Privatization as the Transfer of Public Space or Assets to Individual/Corporations*

There may be some dispute about the definition of privatization employed in this discussion. As Miron and Nelson (2002) indicate in their study of charter schools in Michigan, they employed the concept of a public school or space as it has been used in this book as *formalist*, a definition "which focuses on issues of control and ownership" (p. 195).

*According to this definition, a school (or other institution) is public if it is owned or controlled by citizens or their duly elected representatives. Assessing public-ness with this definition requires an investigation of who owns the means of educational production and to what extent schools and their activities are susceptible to oversight by elected bodies* (p. 195).

Neoliberals and other advocates of privatization would employ a different definition of "public" which Miron and Nelson (2002) labeled a *functionalist* categorization. Within this perspective a school would be "public" if "it performs an important public function" (p. 195). Under this rubric, nearly all private schools, even those operating for a profit, would be public schools as one could argue that an educated citizenry is an expected outcome which benefits society. This approach has been advocated by neoliberal Frederick Hess (2003a) of the American Enterprise Institute. Hess attempts to blur the line between public accountability and privatization citing the case of the Edison Schools who are managing public schools.

This convenient obfuscation of long standing sociological descriptions of different types of organizations (Blau & Scott, 1962) is *rejected* as self-serving to Hess' conservative paymasters at AEI. It is what was meant when Bourdieu (1998) referred to neoliberal ideology as replete with "lexical tricks" which masks a socially conservative ideology palatable because it is categorized by its adherents as "reform" and an advancement instead of a regression.

Parsons (1967) specifically separated the different types of control mechanisms in his general theory of formal organization. Of some importance was what type of agency supervised the managerial authority of the organization. One type of control is simply the general internal norms of an organization and the exercise of general "public opinion". The second type is some sort of what he called "fiduciary board" in a business corporation which was concerned with profit and loss. The third type was what "brings the managerial organization directly into a structure of 'public authority' at some level. In our society this is usually 'political' authority, i.e., some organ of government" (p. 63).

The question of who are the primary beneficiaries of a public versus a private school and especially a private school operating for a profit means that the first beneficiary of such schools are the owners and not the students. Since public schools belong to the public and are accountable to the public via some sort of public authority, the beneficiaries of the school are the students first and foremost.

The neoliberals can't have it both ways. They cannot put their values first on private property and free markets promoting individual choices, and then argue that one should allow owners the right to enjoy property and profits because the common good also benefits. They can survive without the common good being advanced. But they can't survive if their profits don't materialize. Their wealth and welfare must come first. The students come second and the community comes third, if at all, in their ideology. This is a critical and important distinction that is part of the line of argument in this book.

*Step 4: Profitization and the Vagaries and Pitfalls of Making Money*

Once the transfer of public to private has been legislated and enacted, then the new agents intend to make a profit. Corporations that don't make a profit will not survive. That has been a consistent issue with the Edison Project which at 2002 had "never had a profit" (Forelle, 2002, B1).

Two issues come to the fore when privatization has occurred. One is the new mind set which comes to permeate and dominate an organization, in the case of public education, a shift from service as a public good, to reaping a profit with the inevitable corrosive side effects. The second is about making as much money as one can, that is, of making a lot of money.

## The Nature of the Educational Industry and the Rise of the EMO

Anderson & Pini (2011) indicate that "education is a $650 billion industry, making it America's second-largest economic sector" (p. 185) and that the rise of the EMO (Education Management Organization) is an attempt to make money in that sector. To do so requires that the for-profits work in formerly public spaces, something requiring permission from public officials and often legislatures to accomplish.

Pini (2001) analyzed the claims made by EMOs on their webpages and then checked them out with the actual reality of their operations. She found that they claimed to be innovative but used standardized curricula. They claimed to engage in de-bureaucratizing schools but actually were examples of impersonal bureaucracies. They failed to be accountable to the public and teachers in them worked longer hours than their counterparts. Because most of the costs of schools are in staff, EMOs made a profit by employing younger and less experienced teachers and staff. Very similar findings were reported in 2002 in a study of charter schools in Michigan (Miron & Nelson).

Conflict in this arena has occurred in the uneasy tension between the public, public employees and their unions, community representatives, and other elected or appointed public executives. The conservative press regularly backs the *for-profits* as the antidote to "failing schools". A brouhaha in 2002 in Philadelphia with the Edison Schools fell apart over such issues as whether the top 55 district executive jobs would be privatized (McGurn, 2002, p. A22). Edison Schools have failed to live up to their promises and claims enjoying heavy debt and having to settle with the Security Exchange Commission in 2002 for misrepresenting its income. "Edison failed to disclose that as much as 41 percent of its revenue consisted of money that it never saw" (Saltman, 2005, p.55).

According to a report issued by the National Education Policy Center in 2012 there were about 300 private companies functioning as EMOs which operated 35 percent of all public charter schools enrolling more than 40 percent of all charter school students. There were 99 *for-profit* companies in the NEPC's report *Profiles of For-Profit and Nonprofit Education Management Organizations*. Among the *for-profit* companies which included Connections Academy, Imagine Schools, K-12, Inc, Edison Schools Inc., and White Hat Management, the largest was KIPP, operating 109 schools serving 32,000 students in 20 states and Washington, D.C. The total *for-profit* schools administered 758 schools serving about 384,000 pupils. One benchmark of the schools' academic rigor is how many of them met state standards for AYP (adequate yearly progress). The data indicated that only 48.2 percent of the *for-profits* made AYP while the *nonprofit* EMOs did better at 56. 4 percent.

## The *For-Profit* Mindset and its Dangers to the Individual Educational Leader

The *for-profit* orientation is an acquired outlook. It is not innate or as Parsons (1967) notes, "it is not a propensity of human nature" (p. 246). The *for-profit* orientation is comprised of a constellation of values which after a period of exposure and inculcation become personalized to the point where the acquisition of money becomes the greatest good because it becomes the means "available to gratify all need-dispositions with reference to which purchasable means may be important" (Parsons, 1967, p. 244).

The acquisition of money, even when one has money, can become a vicious cycle, especially when money becomes the symbol of prestige and power. There are notable examples of where leaders made very questionable and ultimately business decisions which prove to be detrimental in the long run in the drive to enhance one's compensation.

Take the case of Safeway Chief Executive Steven Burd who got a $2.3 million dollar award based on a "61% jump in the company's per-share profit last year" (Thurm & Ng, 2013, p. B1). The increase in the per profit share did not come about because of any improvement in either job performance by Mr. Burd or sales of the company. Safeway didn't perform any better than it had before. In fact "Safeway's 2012 operating profit fell for a fourth consecutive year. Its stock declined 14%" (Thurm & Ng, 2013, p.B2).

Mr. Burd's bonus came from the practice of buying back stock (normally with borrowed money) which then reduced the number of shares and increased the value of the remaining stock shares. As many corporate leaders are paid by their stock options, the value of the stock went up and when sold by that executive resulted in a handsome, but unearned bonus on the basis of job or company performance. Another CEO, Larry Merlo of CVS, received a $2.8 million three year performance bonus in the same manner as Mr. Burd's.

While critics of paying corporate executives with buyback stock tactics point out it encourages very low goal setting and rewarding short term actions that may not be advantageous in the long run, "nearly a quarter of the 1,500 companies in the S&P stock indexes" employ "per-share earnings [as] the most popular financial-performance yardstick in executive-compensation plans" (Thurm & Ng, 2013, p. B2.). Many of those same companies spent $408 billion on buybacks. One outcome was that while net income grew only 5%, per-share earnings rose 6.1%. Clearly this is a case where CEOs earned money through a practice which was not related to productivity nor their performance.

The *for profit* corporate mindset with what Parsons (1967) has indicated lends itself to the acquisition of power by making money the sole or primary measure of success. When the "making of money" enjoys such a unitary status to the point where it results in the "structuring of the situation of action" (p. 246) the temptation is great to engage in fraud and other forms of cheating.

For example, when Matthew Taylor pled guilty to wire fraud as he tried to hide a $8.3 billion dollar futures bet at the Goldman Sachs Group that went wrong, he tried to conceal his error which cost his firm $118.4 million. Taylor's compensation package for the year in which he was convicted was a base of $150,000 and an expected bonus of $1.6 million (Bray & Baer, 2013, p. C3).

Taylor was a wonder boy. He was class valedictorian in high school and voted "most likely to succeed," went to MIT and was considered a person who achieved his dreams. Taylor confessed in court that, "I accumulated this trading position and concealed it for the purpose of augmenting my reputation at Goldman and increasing my performance-based compensation" (Bray & Baer, 2013, p. C3). Taylor's situation was described by Talcott Parsons (1967) in his book section on the profit motive in *The Social System*, "…the profit motive is a situationally generalized goal, its generality comes from its place *in the definition of the situation,*(italics in the original) and the integration of this with the individual's orientations" (p. 247). In-other-words, the profit motive is an acquired value orientation.

Not only has the for profit motive worked to create a culture of cheating and corruption in the corporate sector which are amply illustrated in this book, but it has begun to do the same in the public education sector as it is being marketized and as states pass legislation to tie teacher and administrator compensation to gains in standardized tests scores (Banchero, 2011a). One very detrimental impact has been the rise of "an autocratic approach to assessment and school leadership that is as damaging to the teaching profession as it is harmful to learning" (Powell, 2011, p. 25)

**Be Aware of Neoliberal "Research": A Legacy of Racism, Elitism, and Half Truths**

Neoliberal think tanks have a long history of cranking out rafts of reports, position papers and research of a most dubious quality. Rarely is such "research" vetted at respectable professional research conferences and even rarer does it appear in the top ranked academic journals in our field. The reason is that it wouldn't pass muster with what is known and that it would be shredded by competent critics.

In 2010 Kevin Welner and Alex Molnar established the National Education Policy Center at the University of Colorado at Boulder (Sparks, 2010, p. 1). The reason for this new venture, according to Kevin Welner co-director of the Think Tank Review project was because, "Across the nation, think tanks are churning out a steady stream of often low-quality reports that use weak research methods, offer biased analyses, and make recommendations that do not fit the data (NEPC, 2010a, p. 1). Similarly, Alex Molnar, a professor at Arizona State University indicates, "...in the political process, the influence of a report often has little relation to its quality. As a result, new school policies and reform proposals frequently are based on research of questionable value" (NEPC, 2010a, p.1).

Two examples come to mind of flawed, biased and racist neoliberal think tank reports. The first is that of the Hernstein and Murray book (1994) *The Bell Curve* from the American Enterprise Institute. The second is from the Heritage Foundation's recent report on how to deal with illegal immigration in the U.S.

*The American Enterprise Institute and The Bell Curve*

The publication of the 1994 book *The Bell Curve* created a media sensation. Conason (2003) summarized the purpose of this work, "Speaking from the commanding heights of the American right, they [referring to Hernstein & Murray] informed the nation that blacks are destined to fail, that racial discrimination is logically and morally defensible as well as natural, and that the government should stop trying to enforce civil rights and help the black underclass" (p. 138).

The sources of data for *The Bell Curve* consisted of "self-proclaimed white supremacists and eugenicists" (Kincheloe & Steinberg, 1997, p.38). Among the most prominent was that of Wycliffe Draper who in 1937 established the Pioneer Fund in order to:

*Promote the procreation of the progeny of white families living in America before the Revolutionary War. The Fund financially supports research that 'proves' that African Americas are disproportionately poor because of their genetic inferiority. Over the last decade the Fund has contributed 3.5 million dollars to researchers cited by Hernstein and Murray* (Kincheloe & Steinberg, 1997, p. 38).

Prominent neoliberals let their class biases, elitism and racism come out. The first is that of AEI Scholar Charles Murray (2005), who like so many other Americans, watched the victims of Hurricane Katrina in New Orleans stream into the New Orleans Superdome to avoid the floodwaters. Murray took the occasion to paint the largely African American victims as a "permanent underclass" where African American males who were not working or even looking for work end up in prison. One cause is the illegitimacy rate which is "heavily concentrated in low-income groups" (A18).

Murray (2005), who once argued against the entire welfare system because it would be better for the poor to be left alone to their own ways (Brock, 2004, p.47), took a similar aim at the plight of the persons Katrina displaced:

> *Versions of every program being proposed in the aftermath of Katrina have been tried before and evaluated. We already know that the programs are mismatched with the characteristics of the underclass. Job training? Unemployment in the underclass is not caused by lack of jobs or of job skills, but by the inability to get up every morning and go to work. A homesteading act? The lack of home ownership is not caused by the inability to save money from meager earnings, but because the concept of thrift is alien. You name it, we've tried it. It doesn't work with the underclass* (A18).

What Murray attributed to the position of the poor economists refer to as the "poverty trap" and it refers to how difficult it is that once one is born into the low income status it is very difficult to leave it (Stiglitz, 2012, p. 20). George Irvin (2008) commented on the poverty trap in the U.K., "A middle class child is 15 times more likely to stay in the middle class than a working-class child is to move into the middle class…A baby's fate is virtually fixed at 22 months. Only the USA has less upward social mobility than the UK among western nations" (p. 205).

Murray's (2005) *Wall Street Journal* op-ed piece essentially blames the victim for his own plight. That is much easier than to address the lack of social mobility in our country generally, which is one of the lowest in the world among wealthy nations (Irvin, 2008, p. 28). "A recent study by the Economic Policy Institute (EPI) in Washington indicates that it would take an average poor family with two children nearly 200 years of economic climbing to attain middle-class status" (Irvin, 2008, p. 28). The racist nature of Murray's remarks were also evident in *The Bell Curve*.

Another prominent neoliberal also got himself into major trouble with a racist remark on his radio talk show. Former U.S. Secretary of Education under Ronald Reagan, William Bennett said, "But I do know that it's true that if you wanted to reduce crime, you could, if that were your sole purpose, you could abort every black baby in this country, and your crime rate would go down" (Borja, 2006, p. 8).

As a consequence of this comment Bennett decided to step down from an EMO he co-founded, K12, Inc. rather than endanger, among other corporation contracts, a $3 million dollar agreement his EMO had with the Philadelphia school system. Murray and Bennett are not the only neoliberals who espouse the outmoded genetic science which consistently posits that African Americans, Hispanics, Native Americans have lower forms of intelligence than whites.

*The Heritage Foundation's Anti-Immigration Dust Up*

Another example is that of the Heritage Foundation's Immigration Report. In the Spring of 2013 as Congress was debating on how to handle the issue of illegal immigration, the Heritage Foundation released a report claiming that immigration reform would cost American taxpayers around $6.3 trillion. The off the wall numbers and assumptions were immediately attacked as spurious by economists and criticized by fellow Republicans. The report was co-authored by Jason Richwine an avowed racist. Richwine had argued that the intelligence of Latino immigrants was "too low" for them to be successfully assimilated into the U.S. (Bouie, 2013, p.12).

*Other Examples of Schlock Neoliberal Think Tank "Research"*

Neoliberal think tanks have resorted to conducting their own "research" and releasing the results directly to the media without ever bothering to vet that research or subject it to the most rigorous review methods within the research community. An unsuspecting and naïve public media establishment rarely has the expertise to critically examine think tank reports and research and often prints it without bothering to seek alternative perspectives or really deal with its flaws, biases, and erroneous conclusions.

The NEPC has examined the quality of some of the neoliberal and other foundations research for rigor and quality. Their reviews have found shocking and egregious errors as well as extremely prejudicial reporting. Some are highlighted here to illustrate the extent to which the reports should be viewed with the greatest skepticism.

In 2010 the Heritage Foundation released a report "Closing the Racial Achievement Gap: Learning from Florida's Reforms" by Matthew Ladner and Lindsey Burke. Madhabi Chatterji, a professor of educational measurement and evaluation at Teachers College, Columbia University reviewed the Heritage report for the NEPC (2010) and found that the "claims…do not withstand scrutiny [and] the report's key conclusions are unwarranted and insufficiently supported by research. One of the reasons was that the effects of Florida's grade-retention policy made the comparisons contained in the Heritage report" largely meaningless" (NEPC, 2010b, p.1)

The NEPC subsequently bestowed upon the Heritage Foundation's report a Bunkum Award for 2010:

> *The award notes Ladner's success in repackaging in many different venues and media his spurious claim that a series of Florida reforms, including tax vouchers and grade retention, 'caused' racial achievement gaps to narrow in the Sunshine State. 'Ladner's fecundity isn't really what sets this work apart. It's his willingness to smash through walls of basic research standards in his dogged pursuit of his policy agenda' according to our judges* (NEPC, 2010c, p. 1).

Another example of very flawed research was that of the 2009 Friedman Foundation called, "A Win-Win Solution: The Empirical Evidence on How Vouchers Affect Public Schools". The Friedman Foundation said that, "…contrary to the widespread claim that vouchers hurt public schools, the empirical evidence consistently supports the conclusion that vouchers improve public schools. No empirical study has ever found that vouchers had a negative impact on public schools" (NEPC, 2011b).

Chris Lubienski, a University of Illinois professor, closely examined the Friedman report and indicated that it "cherry-picks evidence and that the majority of studies cited 'were produced by a very small group of people largely associated with school choice advocacy organizations" (NEPC, 2011b, p.1). In addition this report falsely claims that early studies supported their contention that vouchers had a positive "competition effect" on public school systems when those reports actually said that they found "no competition effect" at all (NEPC, 2011b, p.1).

The Fordham Institute, Chester E. Finn Jr.'s neoliberal bastion in Dayton, Ohio, which is also supported by the Broad Foundation, issued a report entitled "Yearning to Break Free: Ohio Superintendents Speak Out" which was based on a survey of 246 Ohio school superintendents. The report indicated that the "lack of money is not a serious problem for the state's public schools. It also suggests that academic achievement would improve if superintendents were freed from state mandates and teachers' union contracts" (NEPC, 2011c, p. 1).

"Yearning to Break Free" was reviewed by Catherine Horn and Gary Dworkin, both professors at the University of Houston. Horn and Dworkin found that the report's "conclusions are problematic because of the combined effects of non-representative sample, leading or inappropriately worded items, and the conflating of opinion and fact" (NEPC, 2011c, p.1). In addition the response rate was only 40 percent. Horn & Dworkin indicated that as a result of the flaws in this report, it had "little to offer policymakers" (NEPC, 2011c, p.2).

The Fordham Institute has a history of engaging in overblown reports and studies. In 2003 it issued an anonymous blast at educational leadership programs entitled *Better leaders for America's Schools: A Manifesto* which was larded with the standard neoliberal antidotes and criticisms of public education and colleges of education leadership programs. These included arguments for performance pay and the end of licensing of school leaders by opening up the "pipeline" to former generals and corporate leaders, a standard neoliberal argument.

It also reeked of misogyny as these fields have a much lower percentage of females in top positions than educational administration (English, 2004). So the so-called "opening up" of educational leadership positions to persons in other fields dominated by men, represented a "closing down" of leadership positions for women in education. The *Manifesto* was also liberally salted with military metaphors that similarly displayed a gender bias as well as the proclivity of neoliberals to see themselves as combatants instead of consensus builders.

The NEPC external reviews also de-construct and illustrate the myriad ways that think tank research falls remarkably short of acceptable standards of reliability and rigor. Studies by the Progressive Policy Institute on how to grow charter schools using only literature from business literature never explained how that date could be applied to education and fell very short of accepted academic standards was called by David Garcia, the NEPC reviewer as "exponentially flimsy" (NEPC, 2011d, p.1).

Another study conducted by the Gates Foundation on how so-called "value-added analysis" can be used to assess teacher effectiveness was reviewed by Berkeley economist Jesse Rothstein who wrote in his re-examination that the use of value-added models for teacher evaluations actually undermined the call for its increased use (NEPC 2011e). Specifically Rothstein observed:

> *many teachers whose value-added for one test is low are in fact quite effective when judged by the other," [indicating] "that a teacher's value-added for state tests does a poor job of identifying teachers who are effective in a broader sense. A teacher who focuses on important, demanding skills and knowledge that are not tested may be misidentified as ineffective, while a fairly weak teacher who narrows her focus to the state test may be erroneously praised as effective* (NEPC, 2011e, p. 2).

The NEPC external reviews of think tank research should give policy developers, editorial writers, educators, legislators and the general public great pause in passing laws or altering public policy on studies advanced by think tanks whose purpose is to advance a specific cause or solution which they espouse or support. The first criterion of quality research is that the researcher has no vested interest in the outcome of a study and is not an employee or paid consultant to promote or support a specific point of view.

Neoliberal think tanks exist to promote the goals and values of their sponsors, the corporate and individual backers who support them. When foundations such as Gates, Broad and others abandon a neutral position as a true search for what works and instead adopt a venture philanthrocapitalist agenda, the so-called research their foundations and think tanks produce immediately has the taint of self-interest.

That this criterion ought to be obvious is not always the case. For example, the venerable but neoliberal editorial pages of *The Wall Street Journal* reported in a 2011 editorial "Charter and Minority Progress" on "new evidence on school reform and black student progress" in California. *WSJ* gleefully reported a study by the California Charter Schools Association that ostensibly showed that "the average black charter student outscored the average black traditional school student by an average of 18 points over the last four years of publicly available data" (p. A14). The editorial went on to proclaim:

> *The real difference is that charter schools are free of the traditional school system's union contracts and bureaucratic rules, which shorten the school day, stifle innovation and protect ineffective teachers. This autonomy doesn't guarantee charter success, but allows the schools—and their students—to benefit from creativity, competition and accountability* (p. A14).

A different reading of the same data in the CCSA report comes from David Garcia, an expert on charter school research from Arizona State University. Garcia noted that "the data in the report itself show that 'African Americans in California charter schools started out higher and actually lost ground relative to traditional public schools over time' with traditional public schools outgaining charter schools by 6 points" (NEPC, 2011f).

As for the *WSJ* claim about change and charter schools being unfettered to innovate, Garcia noted, "charter schools are of variable quality, and there are very few innovations in charter school practices as a whole that are not also present in traditional public schools" (NEPC, 2011f, p. 2).

*The Wall Street Journal* editorial board has been a long time booster, advocate and proponent of the neoliberal educational agenda. The paper regularly runs op-ed pieces from the neoliberal think tanks as this book illustrates. The *WSJ* can hardly qualify as a neutral observer providing objective editorial commentary on education. They are, to put it mildly, a partisan combatant in this epic struggle.

In summarizing the agendas of the political right and left in America, Brian Barry (2005) saw tremendous success of the right because there is "a network of lavishly financed foundations, and the books and journals that they promote at enormous expense, have rationalized all the most mean-spirited impulses of affluent American whites" (p.233). Further he added, that "…the only honest case that can be made for the agenda of the right is that it suits the people who benefit from it nicely" (p. 234).

# DE-CONSTRUCTING THE CLAIMS OF A L'ENFANT TERRIBLE- ELI BROAD AND HIS NEOLIBERAL EDUCATIONAL CRUSADE

Among neoliberal warriors, none has been more active and outspoken than Eli Broad (Weinberg, 2003; Riley, 2009; Miller 2012; Saltman, 2012). He is truly what the French call a "l'enfant terrible" (the terrible child). His published interviews in the media do not show him to be a particularly deep nor original thinker. He hews to the neoliberal line with fidelity and puts his money where his mouth is.

As Eric Hoffer (1951) observed, "A movement is pioneered by men of words, materialized by fanatics and consolidated by men of action" (p. 134). While Milton Friedman (1962) was a man of words and not a fanatic, Eli Broad is a person of action and a true believer in neoliberal dicta regarding free markets, competition, de-professionalization of leadership preparation in schools of education in the university, anti-teachers union, and the imposition of corporate style management in school districts as a panacea to nearly all the problems urban school systems encounter today. What makes him particularly destructive to public education is that he is terribly rich and has enjoyed a cozy relationship with former U.S. Secretaries of Education Rod Paige (Republican) and Arne Duncan (Democrat), both of whom share much of his prejudices and ideology.

The Broad Foundation supports the Thomas B. Fordham Foundation of Dayton, Ohio, headed by a long time neoliberal roadie Chester E. Finn, Jr. (Maxwell, 2006), and issues a variety of policy papers about education and educational leadership that are congruent with those of Broad himself and his opinions regarding what constitutes educational "reform" (see Thomas B. Fordham Institute & Broad Foundation, 2003).

Among the favorite targets of Finn are schools of education, places "…where ideas originate and get legitimated. They are also where beliefs are held…that fly in the face of common sense, popular preference, and the express will of democratically elected policy makers. They are where the most absurd notions are promulgated…" (Finn, 1991, p. 222).

And what might some of these absurd notions be? After a self-appointed review of two prestigious educational journals produced by Harvard's Graduate School of Education and the Teachers College Record of Teachers College Columbia University, Finn (1991) concluded that "the villains in their pages include racism, homophobia, Eurocentrism, sexism and conservatism" ( p. 225). Finn is critical that these journals reject the ideas of social conservatism, and their aim "…is to reconstruct the society around it" (p.225). Finn is contemptuous of such authors as Henry Giroux (2004), Michael Apple (2006) and Latin American educator Paulo Friere (1970). The problem is from his stance that these writers' "view of the role of education" [is to] "solve…pressing problems of the social order" p. 226).

In a nutshell Finn's critique of a concern for social justice in the larger society is a vacuum. Like Eli Broad and other neoliberals the problem with things like the achievement gap is entirely one of the lack of control and resolve of school leaders and school teachers not cracking down. What the schools need, in his opinion, and that of Broad and his acolytes, is the equivalent of managerial "tough love". The larger societal issues of the growing socio-economic inequalities and how schools perpetuate them and are linked to school achievement (Condron,2011) is never mentioned in their antidotes for urban schools or by their fellow travelers who serve on the *Wall Street Journal*'s editorial board.

Their solutions are simple and passed off as "common sense" (Kumashiro, 2008). Among them are any and all persons or groups who stand in the way of implementation of their pet solutions such as democratically elected school boards, teacher unions and collective bargaining, teacher tenure, licensing requirements, standard salary schedules, leadership preparation in schools of education and schools of education in general (*Table 1*).

The thing that these "barriers" have in common is that they all represent forces of dissent to corporate top-down managerial control and to a successful businessman like Eli Broad who eschews compromise and sees such checks on corporate power as a sell out and a lack of resolve (see Blinder, 2012; Riley, 2009; Weinberg, 2003).

### The Broad Superintendent's Academy

Since 2002 when Eli Broad established the Broad Superintendent's Academy, there have been roughly 146 graduates. Broad brings to his enterprise a disdain for leadership programs in schools of education proffering that they lack the hard management skills and tough minded outlook that contemporary urban school systems require (Ravitch, 2010, p. 213; Broad Foundation & Thomas B. Ford Institute, 2003; English, 2004).

To date, there have been no third party, objective or independent evaluations of the Broad Superintendent's Academy. This section attempts to fill that gap by collecting a track record of the graduates derived from a broad array of Internet and other sources (English & Crowder, 2013). Using the tenets of discourse analysis theory advanced by Halliday (1978) the data reveal discrepancies and distortions in what Broad claims has been accomplished on his website and in the *Broad Foundation 2011-2012 Report*.

### Objectives/Purposes of the Study

The objective of the study, conducted with my graduate assistant Zan Crowder, was to determine if the claims of the Broad Superintendent's Academy and those advanced by Eli Broad himself (Riley, 2009; Ravitch, 2010) could be supported by an examination of the 146 graduates of the Academy and how well they have fared as urban school system leaders. While the Broad Foundation web site does make the names of the Superintendent's Academy public, and also runs related articles/blogs on the success or problems some of the graduates encounter, they do not make public the entire record of the graduates, nor have any longitudinal studies been reported on how well the career records of the graduates have fared. The purpose of the study was to try and fill in the complete picture of Broad's superintendent graduates to determine if the reality was different than that touted by Broad and his Foundation.

### The Perspective/Theoretical Framework

The theoretical framework employed in this review was that of discourse analysis (Gee,1999) which In this particular study was examined as a political practice which "establishes, sustains and changes power relations, and the collective entities (classes, blocks, communities, groups) between which power relations obtain" (see Fairclough, 1992, p. 67) and that of Halliday (1978) who indicated that language within texts is multifunctional because it simultaneously represents reality, establishes social relations, and defines identities. "This theory of language can fruitfully be combined with the emphasis upon socially constructive properties of discourse..." (Fairclough,1992, p. 9).

The Broad website and the information it possesses then can be envisioned as a political practice which is "not only a site of power struggle, but also a stake in the power struggle" (Fairclough, 1992, p. 67). In addition, the theoretical perspective of Pierre Bourdieu of a *field* consisting of a social space in which various actors and agents vie for legitimation and influence was implicit in the analyses, especially the idea that in a professional field if one is to succeed politically, agents or groups must appeal to groups or forces which lie outside that field. Bourdieu (1991) believed that a *field* was relational and dynamic and that it consisted of forces as well as struggles which at any given moment "confers on this field its structure" (p. 171).

As an actor in the current field of power Eli Broad has established himself as a major player (English, 2011; Miller, 2012). Diane Ravitch (2010) has called him one of the "Billionaire Boys Club" (p.195). Eli Broad made his fortune in real estate (KB home) and was founder of SunAmerica, now a subsidiary of AIG. He and his wife Edythe established the Broad Foundation "with the mission of advancing entrepreneurship for the public good in education, science and the arts". The Broad Foundations have assets of $2.1 billion.

According to Wikipedia (2010) "The Eli and Edythe Broad Foundation's education work is focused on dramatically improving urban K-12 education through better governance, management, labor relations and competition." The Broad Foundation has four national flagship initiatives: (1) The $2 million Broad Prize for Urban Education (Samuels, 2011); (2) The Broad Superintendents Academy which is a ten month executive management program to train working CEOs and other top executives from business, non-profit, military, government and education backgrounds to lead urban school systems; (3) the Broad Residency in Urban Education which is a two-year management development program that trains recent graduate students, primarily with business and law degrees, who have several years of work experience and places them immediately into managerial positions in the central operations of urban school districts, and; (4) The Broad Institute for School Boards which is a national training and support program for urban school district governance teams of school board members and superintendents.

**The Method and Modes of Inquiry**

The methods employed for the review were: (a) a content analysis of a variety of largely Internet sources, and; (b) a de-construction of both Broad's claims and the results obtained from the content analysis employing discourse theory. Content analysis is a technique of "answering questions directly relating to the material analyzed" (Borg & Gall, 1989, p. 520) and that "most content-analysis studies are based on data that are already available" (Borg & Gall, 1989, p. 523). Krippendorff (1980) indicates that, "anything connected with the phenomenon that interests the researcher qualifies as data for content analysis" (p.68). Content analysis has also been used in analyzing some of the claims by Broad for deregulating educational leader licensure (Smith, 2008).

De-construction is a tool of discourse analysis. It consists of a double reading of a text (Critchley, 1992). The first reading is merely how any passage or text would be read by the majority of readers. The second reading is a critical analysis of the deeper meanings of a text by what is not there, that is, elements which are missing called *silences* as well as how a line of argument is constructed using binaries and logic. Reading a text for what is not present exposes what the text author did not think important enough to mention or deliberately withheld in the framing of a line of argument. Reaching into a text and recovering the "unthought" or "unspoken" is often a way to show the hidden biases or prejudices in a text and is one of the principal methods of postmodern critique (English, 2013).

The primary source for the content analysis is the website of the Broad Foundations and the *2011-2012 Broad Foundations Report.* We began by determining what claims the Broad Foundation made with regards to their Superintendent Academy and their Residency Programs as well as to the state of public education in general. Once we established these claims, we used numerous sources to investigate their validity. Data were collected through the use of social networking sites such as LinkedIn and Zoominfo which listed resume information for many of the graduates of the Broad Academy.

Articles in the popular press were used to verify information posted on networking sites as were school district websites. From this information, a table was compiled of all Broad graduates with as much of their professional history both prior to and after the Broad training program that could be gleaned from our sources. Numerous other websites including those of state departments of education, private and non-profit foundations and the Broad Foundations' itself provided further corroboration and triangulation.

**The Results of the Study**

The results of the content analysis are shown in the Appendix A attached to this book and viewed through discourse theory indicate that the data challenge the reality claimed on the Broad Foundations website and in other documents produced by Broad's foundations and institutes. (Broad Foundation and Thomas B. Fordham Institute, 2003; English, 2004; English & Crowder, 2012; Saltman, 2012).

Perhaps the most misleading is of the 146 Broad Superintendents Academy graduates, at least 50% were educators before their exposure to the Broad corporate curriculum. By our count, 20% were from the military and 15% from the corporate sector, with 5% from various public administration roles. Of those 146 graduates only 53 (36%) remain in public education leadership positions, but not all in the superintendency.

Further, evidence exists that although the Broad Superintendent's Academy espouses a managerial philosophy derived from private industry and explicitly rejects the training many administrators receive through traditional educational channels, their pool of graduates is largely comprised of individuals who have, in fact, risen through the educational ranks in the traditional educational career trajectory.

The Broad Foundations' initial press release states that many superintendents "have little training or background in complex financial, labor, management, personnel and capitol resource decision-making. In fact, 98 percent of superintendents are trained as teachers— not managers" (The Broad Foundation, 2001). This claim disregards the fact that, although many superintendents did indeed begin their careers in education as teachers, they have also completed numerous courses in educational leadership and administration as required by most states' certification policies.

Finally, the evidence also suggests that graduates of the Broad Superintendent's Academy do not establish a longer tenure than administrators who follow a traditional track, and some have a very sorry record of performance including abrupt terminations and resignations following stormy and controversial tenures if not outright mismanagement. In fact, nearly half of those still working have been on the job less than two years while only nine (17%) have been on the job more than five years.

The webpage of the Broad Fellowship includes a statistic that reads: "86% of Academy graduates are improving student achievement faster than their peers after four or more years as superintendent" (www.broadcenter.org, 2013a). Such a claim allows the Foundation to tout its success while ignoring the fact indicated by our data that very few Broad graduates actually remain in a specific superintendency for as long as four years. This is an emerging trend that our data clearly indicate. The Broad Foundation claims that the Academy "identifies transformation leaders…and prepares them to lead large urban school districts, state departments of education and high growth public charter systems" (www.broadcenter.org, 2013b) but it does not acknowledge that many of its graduates move quickly from one supeintendency to another or to employment outside the public education sector. In fact, our data illustrate that 8 of 146 (6%) are in positions of state leadership.

The Broad Foundations' 2009/10 report indicated that Arne Duncan, currently the U.S. Secretary of Education, had hosted 23 Broad Residents when he served as CEO of the Chicago Public Schools. Now as U.S. Secretary of Education, he has hired five Broad Residents and alumni and in 2009 an Academy Graduate was employed as Assistant Secretary for Elementary and Secondary Education.

Our data also show that 41 of Academy graduates (28%) have gone into consulting/venture/entrepreneurial/nonprofit jobs dealing with education. Of these 41, 23 (56%) moved from a superintendency to the private sector. Broad graduates have a tendency toward short tenures and are increasingly turning from the superintendency toward other educational ventures that are often without the high level of responsibility and scrutiny that accompanies public executive positions.

As much recent analysis of the highly publicized success of the schools of Union City, New Jersey has indicated, education reform is a long-term proposition that requires more than a transformational leader to step in for a few years. As a white paper published on the Broad Foundation's website and entitled, "75 Examples of How Bureaucracy Stands in the Way of America's Students and Teachers" puts it, "Frequent changes in central office and school leadership may halt efforts to address student achievement or slow change" (www.broadcenter.org, 2013c). Our data reveal that short tenures and high turnover are prevalent among Broad graduates and that claims of improved student achievement by Broad graduates are misleading because of the lack of leader longevity.

Interestingly, the Broad Foundation's website, on a page entitled, "Impact of Broad Graduates," highlights the achievements of four of its alumni: Mark Roosevelt, Peter Gorman, Heath Morrison and Lillian Lowery Of these four, two no longer remain in public education. Mark Roosevelt is currently the president of Antioch College and Peter Gorman is employed in the private sector after unexpectedly resigning from the Charlotte-Mecklenburg school superintendency. Heath Morrison, who replaced Gorman, has been the superintendent of Charlotte-Mecklenburg schools since 2012. The Broad website touts

Morrison's impact in raising graduation rates in Washoe County, Nevada but does not mention that his tenure there lasted only three years before he jumped to Charlotte.

Lillian Lowery, the state superintendent of Maryland schools since July, 2012, began her career as an English teacher and climbed through the administrative ranks from principal to central office to superintendency. Her distinguished career is typical of the trend indicated by our data that traditionally trained educators who proceed through the ranks of public education in one general location are the likeliest of Broad alumni to have long tenures and consistent records characterized by lifelong commitment to public education.

**Significance of the Study**

The Broad Superintendent's Academy is an exceptionally well-endowed, highly-connected institution that, at least in the mind of its sponsor, espouses a very particular, market-based ideology with regards to public education (Miller, 2012; Saltman, 2012). Because of the Academy's lack of curricular and procedural transparency, the only recourse left to the researchers was to examine the Broad claims in light of the behaviors of its graduates.

This section was a preliminary study reported at the American Education Research Association in May of 2013 in San Francisco intended to introduce and encourage several different avenues of further research. First, the claims of the Broad Foundations and the Broad Academy, in the interest of public education and traditional leadership training programs, must be interrogated in order to determine their veracity and to reveal their ideological underpinnings. Second, because of the placement of Broad graduates in a large number of urban school districts, continual investigation is warranted as to the efficacy of these graduates in raising achievement and improving educational experiences for the nation's children.

While we concur with the Broad Foundations' assertion that superintendents perform a crucial role in the educational system, and that they are in the position most likely to affect positive change for a given district, we challenge the position that a private academy with the espoused, if not actualized, goal of recruiting executives without educational experience or background is the best way to produce effective leadership.

The preliminary results of our study indicate that a majority of Broad graduates with tenures of three or four years are traditionally trained educators and administrators for whom the benefits of a Broad training program are difficult to ascertain given their prior experiences. Third, what is certain is that graduation from the Broad Academy enables individuals to participate in a network of executive placement both in the public sphere and within private, corporate management organizations. As Broad graduates command an ever increasing share of the educational leadership market, it is of crucial importance that research such as this be conducted in order to investigate these graduates, their educational philosophies and their performance.

Broad's agenda is clear, the de-professionalization of educational leadership at the university level along with a major push to marketize and commodify the field of educational leadership and advance the corporatist reform agenda in America's urban centers. Kenneth Saltman (2012) has trenchantly summarized the Broad agenda as:

> *This is not merely a matter of instituting a corporate style of educational leadership. Such pedagogy also involves teaching future leaders to*

*understand their identities in reference to the private sector rather than to the public sphere, and teaching future leaders about the alleged virtues of privatization schemes such as 'choice' and charter schools (p.66).*

Miller (2012) also notes that, "the Broad Foundation confuses an indicator of equity with the more fundamental construction of an equitable society" (p. 2) while it reduces "...the scope of the field...to an exercise in managerialism" (p. 2). It is because of this fundamental misrecognition that Broad's efforts will not reform anything, but reinforce and expand the social and economic inequities which currently exist in the public schools (English, 2012). Instead of reform what Broad really promises is refinement of the status quo. The corporate, neoliberal agenda for school reform Broad proffers offers little hope for any significant positive improvement of American education. As Monahan (2005) has commented:

*The transformations under way are not merely about the transfer of public resources to private industries; they indicate, instead, the widespread commodification of public education and the production of new forms of life. Neoliberalism, as the dominant expression of globalization in the public sector, colonizes public education with its rationalities and yokes the institution to global capital. When public education scales back its social or civic functions in order to accommodate global expectations and industry needs, it concurrently exerts greater social control on actors in these systems (p. 182).*

Our preliminary content analysis of the career trajectories of the Broad Superintendent's Academy graduates in the main show a very meager overall impact on urban educational centers thus far, though some of its candidates occupy some of the largest and most visible urban school systems in the nation. A small number of Broad graduates are working at state and federal education levels and with the data available it is difficult to assess their actual impact.

Finally, the trend that of those Broad graduates who remain active in education, 38% are now employed in the private and for-profit educational sectors. This should not be surprising given the fact that Broad's entrepreneurial biases within the venture philanthropy assault on public schools come through in the claims made on his websites and in the recruiting of for profit minded candidates who then pursue alternative routes open to them in the private sector after serving brief tenures in the public sphere.

The data from our initial review would suggest then that a significant segment of Broad Academy graduates are not so much interested in improving urban public education by enduring the hard slogging of real change and reform which is involved with improving minority student achievement in those systems, but rather in making money in education as it is increasingly commodified, marketized and profitized.

# THE INSTALLATION OF GREED AS THE RAISON D'ETRE OF LEADERSHIP AND THE RESULTING CULTURE OF CORRUPTION

When former New Orleans Mayor Ray Nagin was indicted on 59 charges of corruption which included bribery, conspiracy, wire fraud, money laundering and filing false tax returns which included setting up a bribery and kickback scheme in which he sold the power of his office for cash gifts, private jet travel, and free limousine rides, few would argue that this definition of corruption was not accurate or warranted (McWhirter, 2013, p. A6). That his actions were prompted by greed, defined as "inordinate or reprehensible acquisitiveness" (Webster's, 1972, p. 366) is unmistakable.

When in the last seven years 32 New York officeholders have been indicted or convicted for mail fraud, theft of public funds and other transgressions, (Orden and Gardiner, 2013) the level of corruption becomes a barometer of the fact that where once the norms may have discouraged such transgressions, they now have been weakened or even changed by becoming either lax or weakly enforced. So it is not just a situation where there are a few bad apples in the barrel, the entire barrel has been infected.

It is instructive to note that in a 236 page report that cost $22.4 million to write on why Barclays bank endured a series of terrible scandals, the consultant, Anthony Salz, said that one of the contributing factors was "… a lack of self-awareness that contributed to the deeply disappointing chapter in Barclays long and proud story. If short-term financial returns and employee rewards are ever too dominate in the bank's culture, problems will result" (Enrich, Patrick & Colchester, 2013, p. C3). Mr. Salz indicated that one of the contributing factors was the "excessive win-at-all-costs culture" (Enrich, Patrick & Colchester, 2013, p. C3).

It is precisely this kind of culture that is being imposed on educational leadership and schools via neoliberal, largely Republican sponsored legislative enactment in many states today. As these laws are implemented we can expect to see some of the same results as in the corporate world.

For example, Cools (2005) studied corporate fraud and found between 1978 through 2002, "federal regulators initiated 585 enforcement actions for financial misrepresentation by publicly traded companies, naming 2,310 individuals and 657 firms as potentially liable parties" (p.B2). The individuals involved were fined $15.9 billion and 190 corporate leaders received jail sentences. In addition companies were fined an additional $8.4 billion along with damages from class action law suits.

Clearly, these figures represent more than a "few" rogue individuals engaging in a random reckless act. In fact, the *Financial Times* (2012) acknowledged the nature of the problem when on its editorial page it observed, "The wrongdoing that has been exposed also points to wider concerns about the wayward behavior of the financial sector. The pursuit of unrealistic returns seems to have entrenched a culture of recklessness" with the recommendation that "A new culture is required at the top of financial institutions" (p. 8).

The kind of cutthroat culture that has come to characterize American corporate life has established a level of cheating and chicanery in which getting caught and having to pay a fine is simply the cost of doing business. This is what Jonathon Yarmis, vice president of disruptive technologies for HIS Research said after Google was fined $22.5 million for placing tracking cookies in Apple's Safari Internet browser in iPads, iPhones and Macs. Observing that Google's profits were in the range of $12.2 billion the fine levied against them "…isn't even a slap on the wrist" (Martin, 2012, 1B). Previously Google had been placed in a twenty year period of review after being caught in another scheme and agreed to the Federal Trade Commission not to mislead consumers anymore. Instead Google quietly "managed to attach cookies in many cases by circumventing Safari's default cookie-blocking setting" (Martin, 2012, p. B1).

So being in business is not only about making money, but making a lot of money, even if it means repeatedly cutting corners and outright cheating. Essentially it's about greed because "Market constraints alone are not always enough to ensure good behavior" (*The Economist*, 2012, p. 64). A study of 283 cartels that were established between the years 1990 and 2005 indicated that by preventing competition, "The aggregate revenue increase [they] achieved by acting as they did was over $300 billion" (*The Economist*, 2012, p. 64).

**Stiglitz' Explanation for the Existence of a Culture of Corruption as the Norm**

The Nobel Prize Winning Economist Joseph Stiglitz (2012) defines the term "rent seeking" as several methods used by the very rich to get richer at the expense of the rest of us (p.39). His analysis begins with how corporations work to make sure that markets don't function well. Corporate leaders take actions to be less transparent, restricting the flow of accurate information in order to keep their customers ignorant about what they are actually doing so that they can prey upon them and wheedle even more profits from them via operational fog.

Corporate leaders also lobby to ensure that there are few, if any, legal restrictions from barring them from engaging in anti-competitive activities, or when there are such barriers, they have plenty of legal loopholes and/or are laxly enforced. Stiglitz (2012) reminds us, " The focus of businesspeople, of course, is not to enhance societal wellbeing broadly understood, or even to make markets more competitive: their objective is simply to make markets work <u>for them</u>, to make them more profitable" (p.35). Here are just a few recent examples of the kind of corporate behavior that represents corruption and cheating which illustrates Stiglitz' benchmarks.

***Lack of transparency and keeping your customers or regulators ignorant in order to take advantage, mislead, deceive or bilk them***

*J.P. Morgan Chase and Company* admitted that "through much of early 2012 the bank didn't give its front-line regulator regular reports about profits and losses…The company has said losses ultimately exceeded $6 billion" (Patterson & Fitzpatrick, 2012, B1). The former chief financial officer conceded "a lack of transparency" following a 301 page report that "slammed J.P. Morgan for misleading investors and regulators" (Patterson & Fitzpatrick, 2012, B1).

*Capital One Financial Corporation* agreed to pay $210 million to resolve issues concerning the matter of having its call-center contractors "… pressure customers into buying consumer-credit-protection products such as identity-theft-monitoring services" (Ricker, Johnson & Zibel, 2012, p. C1). Capital One "will refund $150 million to 2.5 million consumers and pay $60 million in fines—including $25 million to the Consumer Financial Protection Bureau (Ricker, Johnson & Zibel, 2012, p. C1).

In 2011 *GlaxoSmithKline* indicated it would pay the U.S. Government $3 billion to settle claims regarding the diabetes drug Avandia which had been shown to be linked to increased heart attack risks. "A Senate Finance Committee report last year accused Glaxo of knowing for several years about data linking Avandia to cardiovascular risks, but playing down the information and trying to suppress doctors who raised concerns" (Whalen, 2011, p. B3). Some critics of the entire drug industry indicated that while the settlement was large, "It's just a speed bump. It's the cost of doing business" (Whalen, 2011, p. B3). The settlement also involved two other drugs, the anti-depressants Paxil and Wellbutrin which Glaxo engaged in off-label marketing to audiences not approved for use of the drug; withholding important safety data from the U.S. regulator; [and] "the company plied doctors with perks such as free spa treatments, Colorado ski trips, pheasant-hunting jaunts to Europe and Madonna concert tickets" (Whalen, Barrett and Loftus, 2012, p. B1). In addition, the government said that "Glaxo helped prepare an article published in a medical journal in 2001 that falsely reported Paxil had proven effective at treating depression in children in a clinical trial when the trial showed no such thing" (Whalen, Barrett & Loftus, 2012, B1).

In 2011 *Oracle Corporation* agreed to pay a fine of $199.5 million because it "defrauded the U.S. Government on a software contract that involved more than $1 billion in sales…the Justice Department alleged that Oracle misrepresented its discounting practices, causing government customers to receive deals that were inferior to those Oracle gave its corporate customers, contrary to the terms of a 1998 contract" (Worthen, 2011, p. B3).

*Credit card giant American Express* agreed to pay a fine of $112.5 million because "the company charged unlawful late fees, misled consumers on debt collection issues and discriminated against new-account applicants on the basis of age" (Randall & Johnson, 2012, p. A1-2.) The breakdown of the total fine was "$27.5 million in penalties; $14.1 million to the CFPB; $3.9 million to the FDIC; $9 million to the Federal Reserve and $500,000 to the Office of the Comptroller of the Currency" (Randall& Johnson, 2012, p. A1-2).

*Finding loopholes and cutting corners to push profits*

*The biotechnology corporation Amgen* agreed to pay a fine of $762 million for illegally marketing the drug Aranesp. Aranesp "was once Amgen's biggest product, with sales of more than $4 billion a year. Sales have declined since 2007 because studies show that high doses can lead to blood clots and the worsening of cancer…Marshall L. Miller, acting United States attorney in Brooklyn said "Amgen was 'pursuing profits at the risk of patient safety'" (Pollack & Secret, 2012, p. B3).

*United Technologies Corporation's Pratt and Whitney* jet engine manufacturing unit discovered an elaborate and long term practice of faking test data which were used to demonstrate its engines and engine parts met the highest safety standards. The FAA, concerned about such shortcuts, had launched its own investigation regarding the safety of "tens of thousands of engine parts used on popular business jets and turboprop aircraft flown by airlines around the world" (Pasztor, 2013, p. B2.

*Wall-Mart Stores* were fined $352 million in 2008 "to settle 63 suits across the country over allegations that it didn't provide workers with proper rest and meal breaks" and in 2012 agreed to pay employees " $4.8 million in back wages and damages, as well as $464,000 in civil penalties…after the U.S. Department of Labor found the company failed to pay overtime to more than 4,500 workers" (Banjo, 2012, B3).

In 2010 *Hewlett-Packard* agreed to pay a fine of $55 million to the U.S. Government as the result of a U.S. Justice Department's investigation in which "H-P knowingly paid 'influencer-fees' to systems-integrator companies in return for recommendations that federal agencies purchase H-P products" (Kendall & Sherr, 2010, p. B3). Further, the Justice Department claimed that, "H-P's 2002 contract with the General Services Administration for computer equipment and software was defectively priced because the company provided incomplete information to contracting officers during negotiations" (Kendall & Sheer, 2010, p. B3).

*Tiffany's has sued Costco Wholesale Corporation* because "the warehouse chain sold engagement rings it falsely claimed were made by the luxury jewelry company" (Zimmerman, 2013, p. B3). This was not the first such type of suit against Costco. "Costco removed a Pablo Picasso drawing from its website in 2006 when the authenticity of a previous Picasso drawing it sold was questioned. A federal jury in Houston found Costco guilty of trademark violation in 2011 for selling a fake copy of a Farouk Systems Inc. product called a CHI flat iron" (Zimmerman, 2013, p B3).

*Colluding with competitors to keep prices high and avoid free market economies*

*General Electric* agreed to pay a fine of $70 million because of charges that it engaged in bid-rigging on investment contracts for municipalities. Three General Electric employees were sentenced to prison terms and nineteen other persons pled guilty or were convicted of criminal charges. Settlements were also reached with Bank of America, United Bank of Scotland, J.P. Morgan Chase & Co. and Wells Fargo & Wachovia. In pleading for leniency of the court one defendant's lawyer argued that "their clients' alleged behavior was a standard industry practice at the time" (Bray, 2012, C3).

In 2011 France's Autorite de la Concurrence hit *Procter & Gamble, Colgate-Palmolive and Henkel AG* companies with a fine of $484 million for price fixing the cost of soap between 1997 and 2004. According to a 177 page report written by French anti-trust authorities, the purpose of the long running plan was "to limit the intensity of the competition between them and clean up the market" (Colchester & Passariello, 2011, B1).

A fine of $1.92 billion was handed out to such corporations as *Philips Electronics* and *Panasonic Corporations* along with *Samsung* and *Toshiba* for engaging in price fixing from 1996 through 2006 on cathode-ray tubes for installation in televisions and desktop computers (Mock, 2012, p. B1).

*UBS* agreed to pay a fine of $1.5 billion to settle charges that it was involved in bid rigging over interest rates, the so-called Libor rate scandal that involved "trillions of dollars in loans and other financial products" ( Enrich & Eaglesham, 2012, A1).

*Stealing trade secrets from competitors*

A federal jury in Pittsburgh found that computer chip maker *Marvell Technology Group* had infringed on a patent held by Carnegie Mellon University and was given an award of $1.17 billion for willful infringement (Clark, 2012, p. B1).

In 2013 *General Electric* filed a lawsuit against corporate rival Whirlpool Corporation indicating that its rival colluded with two European firms to run "a price-fixing cartel that caused GE to overpay for parts for its refrigerators" (Linebaugh, 2013, p. B7).

In 2011 *Nokia Corporation* filed a complaint with the U.S. International Trade Commission that corporate rival Apple had infringed , "on Nokia patents in virtually all of its products". The infringement involved 46 patents held by Nokia.(Grundberg & Moen, 2011, p. B6).

In a long standing and costly legal fight between *Mattel Corporation and MGA Entertainment* over "...the Bratz dolls[which] were introduced in the fall of 2001 and at the height of their popularity grossed $1 billion in revenue for closely held MGA. The glitzy Bratz girls were also the first serious challengers to Barbie" the U.S. Ninth Circuit Court of Appeals in San Francisco threw out a lower court victory for Mattel which alleged it owned the design for the Bratz dolls. In fighting back MGA, "alleges at least four former Mattel employees, with the knowledge of Mattel executives, disguised themselves as retailers or toy distributors—complete with fake business cards and dummy invoices—to gain access to competitors' show rooms at toy fairs and glean information on rivals' newest products, price lists and marketing strategies" (Zimmerman, 2011, p. B7).

In 2013 *Teva Pharmaceutical Industries Ltd* and *Sun Pharmaceutical Industries Ltd* "agreed to pay $2.15 billion in patent-infringement damages to Pfizer Inc. and Takeda Pharmaceutical Co. for selling low-cost copies of heartburn reliever Protonix before the branded drug's U.S. patent expired ...the settlement is believed to be the highest tab for damages from a so-called at-risk launch of a generic drug, one of the tactics used by generic makers to get copies of big-selling drugs on the market as quickly as possible" (Loftus, 2013, p. B2).

It is clear from these examples that many of the highest managerial levels of the most prestigious corporations in America and abroad have engaged in fraudulent, destructive, corrupt, deceptive practices chasing profits and living in a culture where as David Callahan (2004) incisively remarked, "It is easy to cheat like crazy and yet maintain respect for yourself in a society with pervasive corruption" (p. 174). Despite the fines and new laws there is no sign on the horizon that it will cease any time soon. Indeed the comment by Charles Prince, former Citigroup Chief Executive Officer said in mid-2007, "...as long as the music is playing, you've got to get up and dance. We're still dancing" (Smith, 2010, p. C3).

**The Violation of the Public Benchmarks of Justice and Fairness**

Steven Law, the president and CEO of Crossroads GPS, commented on the IRS flap which erupted in the Spring of 2013 by saying, "Any good CEO will tell you that ethical meltdowns like the IRS political-targeting scandal are rarely the work of a few rogue employees. Such messes are the result of a toxic culture that has been allowed to fester" (Law, 2013, p. A17).

We see the downside of a dominant toxic corporate culture seeped in the scorecard for acceptable behavior defined only by profits in the case of Todd Newman, a former hedge-fund manager with Diamondback Capital Management LLC, who was sent to prison for four and half years for insider trading based on sharing corporate secrets. The U.S. District Judge, Richard Sullivan, noted in sentencing Mr. Newman, "This was all about money and getting more. It's hard to explain how someone would do that where they had so much in their life" (Bray, 2013b, C2).

The same federal judge also sent another hedge fund manager, Anthony Chiasson, to 6 and half years of prison for insider trading that garnered $68 million in illegal profits. The judge "struggled to understand why the 40-year-old defendant engaged in the crime considering he was already "fabulously wealthy" (Bray, 2013c, p. C3). Mr. Chiasson's tax returns indicated that at the time he engaged in the crimes he was earning between $10 million and $23 million a year" (Bray, 2013b, p. C3). The pervasive culture of corruption in business and corporate life is indicated by the fact that since 2009 in only New York City, federal prosecutors and the FBI have secured 73 guilty pleas or convictions from 81 people charged (Bray, 2013b, C2).

The second indicator of how widespread corruption exists is that when the perpetrators are prosecuted and convicted, they and the firms for which they worked pay a fine without admitting that they did anything wrong. Several federal judges have commented on this incongruity. For example, U.S. District Judge Victor Marrero commented that, "There is something counter intuitive and incongruous in a party agreeing to settle a case for $600 million—that might cost $1 million to defend and litigate—if it truly did nothing wrong" (Bray, 2013a, p. C3). Another federal judge, Jed S. Rakoff, rejected a proposed $285 million settlement of civil fraud charges against Citigroup "to which the bank didn't have to admit wrongdoing, saying it was 'neither fair, nor reasonable, nor adequate, nor in the public interest'" (Bray, 2013a, p. C3.).

What these judges are publicly saying in their sentencing of miscreants in the high world of corporate finance revolves around what Sandel (2012) warned when he said that "financial incentives and other market mechanisms can backfire by crowding out nonmarket norms" (p. 114). What has been crowded out is the concept of fairness within the idea of justice. John Rawls (2003) has put a finer point on Sandel's (2012) admonition when he wrote, "…as a social process, justice as fairness focuses first on the basic structure and on the regulations required to maintain background justice over time for all persons equally, whatever their generation or social position" (p. 54).

The basic structure of fairness must apply equally to everyone, *before* it is applied to "particular transactions between individuals and associations" (Rawls, 2003, p. 54). The idea of "background justice" works as a base for a judge making a decision about a specific case. The judge must weigh a particular case in which, in the matter of the settlements, does not violate the political concept of justice as fairness with the full knowledge that, "Very considerable wealth and property may accumulate in a few hands, and these concentrations are likely to undermine fair equality of opportunity, the fair value of political liberties, and so on" (p. 53).

Justice as fairness must deal with the inequalities among citizens and confront them when they are due to social class of origin, native endowments and the opportunity to develop them by social class of origin, and the presence or absence of good fortune or luck. When a plea bargain is reached when those that are guilty use their enormous wealth and political power to secure leniency and avoid accepting their responsibility to the larger society for their actions, Rawls (2003) concept of background justice has been breached. It is to this transgression the judges were reacting.

# THE CULTURE OF CORRUPTION COMES TO K-12 EDUCATION

**The Crooked Future is Already Here Big Time: The Case of *For Profit* Higher Education**

If one wants to see the future of the type of corrupt corporate culture which is coming to K-12 education it's already here and it's just as ugly as what has been cited in the previous prevailing business practices of larger corporate America. To use a business phrase, *the bottom line* is, when education is a business it develops business problems. When education is about making a profit then that's what it becomes first and foremost, a means to make a profit. Everything else becomes secondary. And one can forget abiding by laws, rules, or ethical conduct in the process. It's just about making money, period.

This point was underscored by Thomas Wolanin, a former Democratic Congressional aide who helped manage three previous renewals of the Higher Education Act. "It's all about politics and power, and who gets money, and not about broad discussions of public policy. And Democrats are not much better than Republicans on this score" (Burd, 2004, p. A16).

As the tenets of neoliberalism and the installation of corporate management are being applied to elementary and secondary education, the on-line for profit market in higher education has come under increasing scrutiny for unethical and rule flouting practices. In 2010 the for- profit universities were enrolling about 7 percent of the 19 million students in all degree granting institutions (Wilson, 2010, p.A1). "Of the roughly 3,000 for-profit institutions, 40 percent are now owned by one of 13 large, publicly traded companies" (Wilson, 2010, p. A16).

The largest of these are by annual revenue for fiscal year ending in 2004-05:

1. The Apollo Group (The University of Phoenix) $2.25 billion
2. Career Education- $1.76 billion
3. Education Management- $1.02 billion
4. Corinthian Colleges-$963.6 million
5. DeVry-$781.3 million
6. Laureate Education- $648 million
7. ITT Educational Services-$617.8 million
8. Strayer Education-$183.2 million (*The Chronicle of Higher Education,* 2005, p. A31).

In the 2010 academic year, " the University of Phoenix eclipsed California State University as the second largest higher-education system in the country with 455,600 students as of this month—behind only the State University of New York" (Wilson, 2010, A1).

The for-profit colleges charge more than public colleges, "an average of $14,174 this year [2010] compared with $2,544 at public two year institutions and $7,020 for in-state tuition at public four-year institutions, according to the College Board" (Wilson, 2010, A19). If any industry ever depended on the largesse of government to make it profitable it is the for-profit college market. Government revenue for the Apollo group was 86% in 2009 and 80% for Career Education in the same year (Winkler, 2010, p. B16). By marketing to low-income students who when accepted, often without submitting any transcripts or undergoing any review for ability to engage in college work, they then helped the students qualify for government assisted aid. According to Winkler (2010), from 2000 to 2009 "taxpayer-guaranteed loans and grants flowing to the industry leapt, to $26.5 billion from $4.6 billion" (p. B16).

The problem for the for-profits is that the cost of the degree they charge is often more than the jobs their students could actually earn in the real job market, making it unlikely they would or could pay the loans back. For example, according to Kelly Flynn of CreditSuisse, a two year associate degree from ITT cost about $47,000. But the average starting salary for graduates who become employed is only $30,000 assuming they all could get jobs. The loan default rate is about 24%. This is a situation where corruption and fraudulent practices are bound to emerge, just as in the business for-profit corporate sector.

For example, in 2004 The Apollo group was fined $9.8 million by the U.S. Department of Education because University of Phoenix recruiters "worked in a high-pressure sales environment and were paid solely according to how many students they enrolled" (Borja, 2004, p. 8). This practice is in violation of U.S. Department of Education rules. A 45 page report from the U.S. Education Department said, "Many [recruiters] expressed that while UOP at one time focused on the student and stressed ethical conduct, the culture now is one where the emphasis is on increasing numbers, the stock price, and meeting Wall Street's expectations" (Borja, 2004, p. 8).

The U.S. Education Department report also indicated that UOP recruiters were pressured into enrolling students who were academically unqualified and to use federal financial aid 'as a tool for closing a sale' (Blumenstyk, 2004, p.A1). The 60 recruiters interviewed told of intimidation techniques where those that had low numbers were stuck in a glass enclosed "red room" where they were subjected to very close supervision and their calls were monitored. Successful recruiters received trips and bonuses, one reporting a trip to Las Vegas with $100 in gambling chips (Blumenstyk, 2004, p. A27). And as for the $9.8 million fine the University of Phoenix had to pay, compared to annual revenues close to $1.8 billion, "one stock analyst noted, the money paid by Apollo is 'chump change'" (Blumenstyk, 2004, p. A29).

In 2004 the University of Phoenix was not the only for-profit college under investigation and lawsuits. The U.S. Department of Justice was investigating the Career Education Corporation and the ITT Education Services. The U.S. Securities and Exchange Commission was investigating Career Education, ITT and Corinthian Colleges. The U.S. Department of Education had imposed restrictions on Corinthian's Bryman College regarding loans and grants. The California Attorney General was investigating ITT for fraud and the California consumer-protection division was examining Corinthian.

The Southern Association of Colleges and Schools put Career Education's American InterContinental University "on warning" because of violations on the criterion pertaining to "institutional effectiveness" and the Accrediting Commission for Community and Junior Colleges of the Western Association of Schools and Colleges, placed two campuses of Career Education's Brooks College on probation. There's more.

There were also class-action lawsuits filed by shareholders of ITT and Career Education accusing those companies of "using misleading financial information to artificially inflate the value of their stock" (*The Chronicle of Higher Education*, 2004, p. A29) and students at Florida Metropolitan University, owned by Corinthian, were seeking class certification regarding their claims that FMU misled them about the transferability of credits from that institution. Also in 2004 ten campuses run by ITT were raided by the FBI (Woods, 2006, p. B10).

By 2010 not much had changed. A new government report on recruiting techniques in the for-profit higher education industry revealed that some "counselors" instructed a potential applicant "to fabricate three dependents on an aid form so that he might qualify for a federal grant…A small D.C. beauty college told an applicant that barbers can make $150,000 to $250,000 a year" ( de Vise, 2010, p. A2). A 18 page report conducted by the Government Accounting Office said, "Of the 15 unnamed colleges targeted in the investigation, four 'encouraged fraudulent practices' and 'all 15 made deceptive or otherwise questionable statements to the GAO's undercover applicants" (de Vise, 2010, p. A2).

In 2011 the U.S. Justice Department and four states (California, Florida, Illinois and Indiana) sued Education Management Corporation for falsely certifying "that it was eligible to participate in federal student loan programs" (Kendall, 2011, p. B2). The schools involved were the Art Institutes, Argosy University and Brown Mackie College.

An anonymous and former faculty member at a for-profit college wrote the following which appeared in *The Chronicle of Higher Education*:

> *My four years of experience as a professor at a for-profit college revealed that the for-profit higher-education industry really is as corrupt as everyone suspects. In my position, I suffered a death threat from a student, was threatened by students and their friends countless times, was publicly denigrated by the administration whenever I raised a question or objected to a corrupt practice, and was continually undermined by a faculty and administration driven by fear and adherence to low standards. My colleagues and I have tolerated drunk and disorderly students in our classes, have been told that students should be allowed to talk on their phones, text, and eat hot meals during class—just to keep bodies in the seats* (Anonymous, 2011, p. B12).

This former for-profit instructor went on to described how faculty are pressured to pass students, to work with "illiterate students", to routinely ignore obvious plagiarism and cheating and "give passing grades to inadequate students, in order to continue bringing home paychecks" (Anonymous, 2011, p. B12). The former professor reported that, "These companies that run these colleges, however will not blink an eye at my departure, or at the plight of the thousands of students left holding the bag…They will keep putting profits before students, selling shares in their companies, and proclaiming that they are 'helping' Americans improve their lives. And millions of Americans will keep falling for their lies" (Anonymous, 2011, p. B13)

There have been several attempts to attack the problems of the for-profit colleges. The first is a rule which has been called the "90/10" index. This metric was created in 1992 in the reauthorization of the Higher Education Act in order "to crack down on fly-by-night institutions that had been set up to reap profits from student-aid programs." (Field, 2011, p. A23). The for-profits fought this rule and complained that it "drives up tuition and penalizes colleges for educating low-income students. Congress has relaxed the rule several times but has refused to eliminate it" (Field, 2011a, p. A23).

The counter strategy that some of the for-profits have taken is to charge more tuition and give students loans themselves even though the default rate is "more than 50%" (Blumenstyk, 2011, A1). There is also a loophole in that the restriction doesn't count GI Bill benefits or federal tuition assistance for active duty military. There has been talk from Congressional legislators to close this gap so that all federal aid is counted in the 90% calculation. The for-profits have lobbied hard to prevent this development.

Perhaps the most controversial approach to regulating the for-profits is a U.S. Education Department benchmark that in order to keep receiving federal funds at all, each proprietary school would have to show compliance of at least one of three criteria. The first was that at least 35% of recent graduates had to repay their loans. The second was the loan repayments could not count for more than 12% of a graduates' annual earnings. The third was that loan repayments would not take up more than 30% of a graduate's discretionary income.

The response was that for-profit "colleges have spent hundreds of thousands of dollars lobbying Congress and federal agencies. Some of the most vulnerable companies spent three or four times as much on lobbying in the second quarter of 2010 than in the same period in 2009. One company, Education Management Corporation, spent eight times as much" ( Field, 2010, A1). This new benchmark began to separate out some of the very bad actors in the for-profit college field (Korn, 2010, p. B6).

The U.S. Department of Education indicated that 48% of the for-profit institutions failed to meet the 35% repayment rate for recent graduates. Among public and nonprofit institutions, only 18% of schools fell short of the same measure" (Belkin, 2012, A3). Another issue is that when a two year versus a three year loan default rate was calculated, which the new Federal law requires, "most of them for for-profit, the three-year default rate is inordinately greater than the two-year rate, giving credence to concerns that certain colleges are aggressively using 'default management' tools to mask problematic rates of default" (Blumenstyk & Richards, 2011, p. A1). In fact, *The Chronicle of Higher Education* examined the data at 243 colleges, or about 8 percent of a total of 3,168 degree-granting institutions and found that the three-year default rate was at least 15 percentage points greater than the two-year figure. "Of those, 83 percent were for for-profit colleges" (2011a, p. A1).

Other information about the for-profits indicates that while the for-profit colleges do increase access for some students to higher education but that "the payoff can be meager. In fact, graduates of for-profit colleges' two-year programs earn about the same as those who finish only high school" (Berrett, 2013, p. A17). Some other for-profit claims are also disputable. For example, some of the for-profits say that their graduation rates are higher than the national average. Yet the fact is that the for-profits calculate their own graduation rates and there is no universally agreed upon method for engaging in such calculations. The University of Phoenix claims that its six-year bachelor's graduation rate is 5.1%, "but that measures fewer than 1 percent of its more than 253,000 students" (Blumenstyk, 2012, p. A14).

Graduation rates are not the only area where the for-profits show major discrepancies. Another area is in the reporting of job placements. In California, the Los Angeles Recording School reported that it had a job placement record of 70 percent. "But a class-action lawsuit says those numbers are a fantasy designed to dupe prospective students and its accreditor" (Field, 2011b, p. A1, A10). While the federal government requires colleges to have their placement rates annually audited, some accreditors are very lax about their procedures and only perform such audits every three to five years. However in 2007 the California attorney general agreed to settle a lawsuit with Corinthian Colleges "that accused it of overstating the percentage of students who obtained employment and of exaggerating their starting salaries" (Field, 2011b, p. A10.)

The new benchmark for the for-profits has been hard fought. On one hand, the non-profits report that "forty-three percent of students attending for-profits are from minority groups, and almost 50 percent are among the first generation in their families to pursue higher education" (Field,2010, p. A17). On-the-other hand is an emerging body of evidence that to keep enrollment numbers high, for-profit "administrators would pressure to falsify attendance records, raise grades, and manipulate job-placement numbers. If a professor refused to change a student's grade, the professor's supervisor would do it, the faculty members say" (Field, 2011b, p. A1). "Faculty members from six of the seven largest publicly traded companies---say they were pressured to raise grades, tolerate plagiarism, and dumb down courses to keep federal student aid flowing" (*The Chronicle of Higher Education*, 2011b p. A10).

One professor said that she had been told by administrators that they "weren't 'fun' enough, that they should engage students through games like Bingo and Jeopardy. To encourage students to show up for class, the college would throw pizza parties and ice-cream socials, and hold raffles for iPods and gift cards" (Field, 2011, p.A10). Finally this professor was told by another, "You know what your problem is? You think you're here to teach" (Field, 2011b, p. A10).

Recently the U.S. Department of Education's new standards suffered a setback when Judge Rudolph Contreras of the U.S. District Court for the District of Columbia said that the proposed debt measures "'lacked a reasoned basis' and called them 'arbitrary and capricious'" and invalidated them (Belkin, 2012, p. A3). However, the judge agreed that the field needs regulation.

And recent enrollment data seems to indicate that potential students are returning to more traditional non-profit schools "and growing skepticism about the value of a high-cost education. Just last week, industry bellwether Apollo said it would close nearly half of its brick-and-mortar locations to save on overhead" (Korn, 2012,p. B1). And the days are over when, according to Kevin Kinser, an associate professor at SUNY Albany, "You could be quite profitable as a business, even when you weren't successful as an educational institution" (Korn, 2012, p. B1).

It is this specter that awaits the elementary and secondary education field as the number of EMOs expand along with charter schools and the installation of other neoliberal policies and educational practices and so-called value added practices. There is every reason to believe, and little doubt, that the corruption of a former public field and its orientation to rendering a service for all children and of operating with transparency and accountability will be at risk. The for-profit higher education industry has shown the way. The loss of civic humanism and the ethic of public service is huge and deeply corrupting of the common good, accentuating the trend towards larger social inequality in which the U.S. leads the world not only in the wealth gap, but in the educational achievement gap which emerging research is beginning to indicate are correlated (see Condron, 2011; Sahlberg, 2011).

As a final note on the coming profitization of the education market and its implications for educational leadership there is the case of Robert Shireman, former deputy undersecretary of education who is now being accused of violating executive-branch ethics laws by discussing inside information with a private group, the Institute for College Access & Success, or TICAS.

Mr. Shireman is accused of sharing information with TICAS regarding a forthcoming push to deal with for-profit colleagues. Mr. Shireman had communication with TICAS through emails that linked individuals in an investment-research firm with "bearish bets on stocks of for-profit colleges and shared information about the industry with senior Education Department officials (Mullins, 2013, p. A6). Finally, when "the department made public the final regulations on July 23, 2010, the rules were weaker than expected, and the stocks of some for-profit colleges rose as much as 15% that day" (Mullins, 2013, p. A6).

Stiglitz (2012) has remarked on the sorry situation of the for-profits:

*But there is one thing that can be done quickly: the for-profit schools, whether financed by government loans, government-guaranteed loans or private loans, with the noose of non dischargeability, have failed to increase opportunity, and have in fact been a major fore dragging down poor aspiring Americans...It is unconscionable that we allow this predatory activity to continue, and even more unconscionable that it is, in effect, supported by public money. Public money should be used to expand support for state and nonprofit higher educational systems and to provide scholarships to ensure that the poor have access* (p. 275).

The ugliness and outright crassness of the for-profit higher education sector continues to rip off many Americans who still believe in the educational ladder to a better life. Whatever silver lining exists there is completely lost in a culture of dishonesty and greed, and until it is cleansed from those evils the odor from that sector will deny it legitimacy and any ethical future on which reputations are gained or lost.

I now move to a consideration of corruption in the K-12 education sector.

**"Kick Ass" Management and the Proliferation of the School Cheating Scandals**

The exemplary models of management being pushed on public education by neoliberal reformers, and touted in the neoliberal press as exemplars are those which could be characterized as hard-nosed, bottom-line, no excuses, *win-at-all-costs management by the numbers* who see the Donald Trump "your fired" line as their calling card.

They are the new exemplars of how to "transform" low performing schools (McGurn, 2010). Neoliberal educational managers see themselves as going to "war" (Klein, 2011) and their work occurring on "battlefields" (Feith, 2012), which means primarily keeping teacher unions, viewed as the neoliberal equivalent of domestic Taliban, from blocking their efforts at "reform" (Klein, 2010, 2011).

I will argue that this approach, advanced by business moguls, neoconservative think tank policy wonks, some neoliberal newspaper columnists and foundation funders Eli Broad and Bill Gates and their directors working to erase the idea of educational leadership as a form of public service based on consensus building, fairness and trust, have succeeded into changing educational leadership into a self-serving platform for personal aggrandizement.

Secondly, branding these heavy handed ideological changes as "reforms" is a hoax, and finally both the methods and means employed to implement them have little to do with "transformational" leadership, a term found frequently in neoliberal commentaries and exhortations. As originally used by James McGregor Burns (1978) it was a term which described the creation of a win-win model of leadership based on mutual respect of the interests of key parties and the creation of a joint venture of change roughly based on participatory parity, i.e., more or less democratic means.

Instead, the corporate neoliberals have appropriated "transformational leadership" to mean a leader who ruthlessly implements top-down change and takes no prisoners in the process, essentially employing a "kick ass" and "take names" fear driven model of bureaucratic manipulation and control. This approach is not even transactional. It is dictatorial and amoral.

The neoliberals cast their aims and their ideological agenda as "reforms." By using "reform" as word to mask their ideological purposes, the lexical camouflage gives their platform an aura of neutrality and when they are defeated it automatically slaps their opponents in the image of enemies of progress. Who can be against reform accept those who like the status quo?

The neoliberal agenda is not a reform at all. Rather it is a specific socio-political-economic regressive change propelled by the drive to turn public space into private space in order to turn a profit. In the words of Joel Klein (2011), former businessman, New York Public Schools Chancellor, and now back to running a for profit technological division for Rupert Murdoch's News Corporation, "Traditional schools and the unions have been screaming bloody murder, which is a good sign: It means that the monopolists are beginning to feel the effects of competition" (p. A15). This remark is a typical neoliberal "reform" that is, that non-privatized public space is evil since it represents a "monopoly."

The contrasts between the culture of business and being a public official such as a school principal or superintendent are striking. Nolan Bushnell, the business man who founded Atari and the Chuck E. Cheese chain remarked that, "Business is a good game—lots of competition and a minimum of rules. You keep score with money" (Blinder, 2012, p. A19). Other contrasts are that political leaders must be concerned with matters of equity and fairness. Again, Blinder (2012) comments:

*Fair dealing can be important in the business world, too. But fairness per se—in the sense of everyone getting his or her just deserts---rarely is. Markets are engines of efficiency, not fairness. In fact, a generous helping of greed may be good in business...*(p. A19).

**Michelle Rhee and the Washington, D.C. "*Your fired*" Neoliberal Playbook**

The rise of the corporate leader who sees dissent and unions as foes to be defeated on public battlefields and refers to their struggle as being "on the barricades" (Feith, 2012) has already produced decisive defeats for such leaders as Michelle Rhee in Washington, D.C., the poster superintendent for "kick ass" management, pro voucher and pro charter, anti-union, linking student test scores to teacher and principal bonuses for test results while firing hundreds of teachers and many principals because of low test scores (Banchero, 2010, 2011c).

The results of Rhee's approach in which, "She refused to believe she needed to build consensus, seek community input or involvement, or in any way inspire or rally the professionals who do the daily work of making school improvements" (Plitt, 2011) were a strong repetition of Enron's infamous "rank and yank" payment plan that created a culture of cutthroat competition, cheating and corruption that ultimately resulted in the company's disgraces and collapse (Callahan, 2004). Rhee's similar draconian style of management also resulted in attrition. After three years as superintendent in the school system, only 55% of the employees who had been there before her arrival remained (Sullo, 2011). They had been "yanked."

When a review of test scores by *USA Today* revealed massive answer changes on test bubble sheets which were clearly above and beyond normal practices, the specter of cheating was raised on a massive scale in D.C. (Gillum & Bello, 2011). Rhee resigned her position when the Mayor who had backed her lost his bid for re-election. Her policies and her management methods were the centerpiece of a very hard fought local election.

After the test score scandal arose it became clear that her rigid run the schools "by the numbers" and reward and punish corporate methods undid her. Remarked one observer, "The climate of fear she created contributed to the obsession of those who might have cheated. The pressure to raise test scores and meet targeted performance goals is very tough. It requires school wide collaboration and hard work. Apparently, some in Washington succumbed to the pressure" (Plitt, 2011, p.1).

**Lorenzo Garcia: The El Paso Miracle Man Becomes The First School Superintendent Sent to the Slammer for Fake Test Score Gains**

Lorenzo Garcia is the first school superintendent in the nation to be sentenced to a three year federal prison sentence for hatching and implementing a large test score fraud that resulted in him earning a $56,000 bonus. He was hailed for his leadership and was twice nominated for the Texas school superintendent of the year for what at first appeared to be an educational miracle.

The cheating scheme involved several school principals and assistant principals, one of whom resigned later while others were reinstated and put on a "two year growth plan" by the board of trustees after the fraud was uncovered (Hinojosa, 2013). The chosen methods to improve test scores were a combination of forcing some students to quit school so they would not be tested at all; altering grades so some students would graduate; and then not testing the lowest performing tenth graders. The "results" were dramatic and instant. One school went from "failing" to "academically acceptable" quickly.

By forcing students to leave school, one El Paso teacher said, "Kids were denied an education and educators just stood by" (Sanchez, 2013, p.4). The lost students involved in

Garcia's crooked plan are called "los desaparecidos" or the "disappeared ones", or "some say 'the forgotten. Officially, 77 kids who dropped out. Investigators say there were probably many more" (Sanchez, 2013, p. 4). The culture of fear created in El Paso can be laid at the superintendent's feet directly. The Director of Student Services , Emanuel Mendoza, who was the whistle blower that brought the fraudulent scheme to light said, "If you said no to him, you were gone" (Sanchez, 2013, p.2).

**Beverly Hall, Maven of Bonus Pay and the Pervasive Culture of Cheating in Atlanta**

And then there is the case of Beverly Hall, the 12 year Superintendent of Schools and former AASA Superintendent of the Year, of Atlanta, Georgia, "who is accused of creating a high-pressure atmosphere where teachers and administrators felt compelled to cheat, and of helping cover up evidence of wrongdoing. Authorities indicted Ms., Hall and 34 teachers and staff in the alleged conspiracy" (Banchero & McWhirter, 2013, p. A6).

A 413 page report completed under the direction of a former state attorney general and a former district attorney "uncovered cheating by students in 44 schools, covering 1,508 classes—almost all of them serving low-income, minority students" (Wingfield, 2011, p. A11). The report labels their findings "a pervasive culture of cheating" (Wingfield, 2011, p. A11). What a "pervasive culture of cheating" actually means as the Georgia Bureau of Investigation conducted its review involved 5 educators terminated after a tribunal hearing; 50 letters sent to educators outlining charges and the school district's intent to terminate; 32 educators notified their contracts would not be renewed, and 39 educators who resigned or retired (Saario, 2012, p. B6).

Ms. Hall earned six figures in performance bonuses for this long running scam, which began in early 2001. Eventually it evolved into a scheme involving many schools where "cheating parties" were held. In 2009 Ms. Hall's total pay was $400,298 which included a car and a bonus for test score gains of $78,115. Her total compensation package that year was estimated at 30 times the amount spent per student in the entire school system."The story in Atlanta is about race, gender, poverty, social class, and of course power. It's about fairness and integrity, about leadership and about failures of leadership, and it's also about social responsibilities and the abdication of that responsibility." (Powell, 2011, p.30).

Part of the neoliberal agenda has been to link teacher pay to standardized test scores. Over half the states in the nation now require tying teacher evaluations to pupil test performance and some include such data in tenure decisions (Banchero, 2011c). The Gates Foundation has been funding an effort to create improved teacher evaluation systems which will accelerate this trend (Gates & Gates, 2011).

Accompanying these developments has been the installation of a "management by the numbers" with a "no-excuses" managerialism that the data produced by the new systems will be used to reward and punish primarily and only secondarily, if at all, as a source for the improvement of teaching. The culture of cheating that has led to other scandals in Philadelphia, Baltimore, New York, Chicago and Los Angeles has been the product of a culture of fear and intimidation built on the false assumption that schools and the leaders and teachers in them control all of the variables to close the achievement gap and enable all children to be successful in them.

This assumption is false because it fails to deal with all of the other factors which should be employed to create a viable social safety net that has demonstrated remarkable results in Finland (see Sahlberg, 2011), but one that is eschewed by neoliberals because it represents an extension of government services to the poor and does not involve the creation of markets where profits can be made with the commodification of public space.

The terrible downside to the neoliberal assault on public education is that, "For many superintendents and principals around the country, there is only one goal to be pursued and achieved; evidence of 'increased student achievement' no matter the means utilized and without regard for unintended consequences" (Powell, 2011, p. 30).

Sol Stern (2013) warns that, "Beverly Hall put 'unrelenting pressure' on schools to drive up test scores by any possible means and that she got $580,000 in performance bonuses as a result…As educators cheat to achieve unrealistic goals, politicians 'are happy to look the other way.' It's a recipe for corruption—and the victims are our children" (p. 10).

That anyone should be surprised with the expanding culture of cheating and corruption in education should simply take a glance at the private, corporate sector where such behavior is much more commonplace and long standing. For example, in 2007 Dell Inc announced that it would have to restate four years of reported profits by $50 million to $150 million because "unidentified senior executives took part in improper actions to hit quarterly performance goals" (Lawton & Clark, 2007, p. A3).

That such behavior has arrived big-time in education should be obvious. And just as the senior executives at Dell, or at any corporation, are rarely in control of all the variables impacting performance and so with impossible goals they resort to cheating. Educational executives are in the same quandary. The fact is that while school is the place where some aspects of educational attainment are measured, however imperfectly that may be, the school does not control all of the variables which determine student achievement.

**The School/Society Nexus and the Achievement Gap**

It is becoming more and more apparent that educational attainment is as much a factor of the home environment, the community context, and other aspects of social and cultural capital in a young person's life as the physical schooling site. The achievement gap is present at age 22 months (see Barry, 2005). The gap cannot be erased until the school/society nexus is considered as "the place" where it is to be confronted (Rothstein, 2004; Wilkinson & Pickett, 2009).

Leaving the larger social issues out of the equation for educational attainment is to be rewarding or punishing the parties who are not accountable for all of the critical decisions regarding educational achievement. If they are totally accountable, but not actually in control of the factors upon which they are going to be held accountable, rewarded or punished, cheating becomes a logical (however unethical) way out of this dilemma. When the goal is unattainable, no matter how cutthroat the management, no matter how draconian the measures the threats and intimidation, the goals will remain unreachable. Cheating is inevitable and will remain a permanent problem in our schools.

However, the neoliberal ideologues will raise all sorts of objections to moving beyond the current socio-political boundaries as their bent has been to reduce or remove the range of social services available to the poor. Since the poor are almost always the ones most dependent on government social services, the neoliberal rant about "big government" (except for the military) amounts to keeping the poor poor. It also means that the achievement gap will be around for a long time, not only in the U.S. but other countries where the difference between the haves and have nots is becoming larger (see Rothstein, 2004; Irwin, 2008; Condron, 2011).

The neoliberal ideological frame not only fixes all "the blame" on the schools, but erects barriers to actually dealing with the social arena where the problems could really be realistically confronted and resolved. The neoliberals need to be "called out" and made responsible and accountable for their blindness in perpetuating the conditions they say they want to resolve.

A good example is Joel Klein's (2011) statement in his op-ed piece in *The Wall Street Journal* in which he wrote:

> *Consider the common refrain that 'We'll never fix education until we fix poverty.' This lets school systems off the hook. Of course money, a stable family and strong values typically make it easier to educate a child. But we now know that, keeping those things constant, certain schools can get dramatically different outcomes with the same kids* (p. A15).

While the former New York City Schools Chancellor and now Rupert Murdoch's chief executive officer in charge of News Corporation's educational technology business, acknowledges the impact of social, economic and cultural capitals that poverty (defined as the lack or absence of those forms of capital) does indeed make a difference, he magically removes their impact by saying "keeping those things constant" poverty can be overcome. How can that happen when it is impossible to keep poverty constant?

The fact is that poverty is growing larger and larger, and the U.S. has one of the largest wealth gaps in the world (see Wilkinson & Pickett 2009; Stiglitz, 2012). Furthermore, keeping them constant would be to preserve the enormous wealth gap which already exists. As for poverty it is but a symptom and not the cause. The cause is the maldistribution of wealth and the way the neoliberals and the 1% have worked at crafting a system of taxation in which they benefit at the expense of the middle and lower classes (see Hacker & Pierson, 2010).

A "fix the schools" focus utterly removes the responsibility of the politicians from dealing with the larger social issues to which the schools are inexorably connected. It's a blame game in which the victims and those who are actually working in them trying to make schools better are subjected to constant criticism for which the solution is beyond their control.

The resolution involves the concept of social justice (Barry, 2005), a term one will never find in neoliberal proposals except to denigrate. But what it means is that if we are actually serious about confronting educational attainment issues we must examine *all* of the factors which contribute to them. At the moment those factors connected to the wealth gap go largely unexamined and excused by the neoliberal think tank writers, their so-called "research" studies, and their ideological home grown remedies for "fixing" the schools.

Changing the schools without changing the socio-economic structure in which they function is to continue to deal with symptoms and not the cause of their problems (Wilkinson & Pickett, 2009). It is doubtful that there is sufficient reflexivity on their part to face up to their own shortcomings other than Joel Klein's (2012) "I should have been more confrontational" swan song as the former Chancellor of the New York City Schools.

# THE AGE OF GREED AND THE IRON CAGE OF SCHOOLING

The Weberian "iron cage" metaphor aptly describes what is occurring in American education today and indeed, in many other countries infatuated with the tenets of neoliberalism (see Mullen, Samier, Brindley, English & Carr, 2012). Up to this point this book has been concerned with what Pierre Bourdieu (2008b) has identified as "the ideological apparatus" of neoliberalism in which he observed that, "The most successful ideological effects are those that have no need for words, and ask no more than complicitous silence" (p. 188).

It has been the purpose of the text to this point to unmask and to de-construct the silence around how neoliberals and their think tanked networks and foundations, are working to change American public education and package their rejection of the common school and its idealism with that of corporate privatization of public space cleverly disguised as a "reform."

If we but take a look at the separate initiatives and put them together, it is possible to see the iron cage being constructed right before our eyes. We only need to see how all of the pieces come together. These are shown in Figure 2.

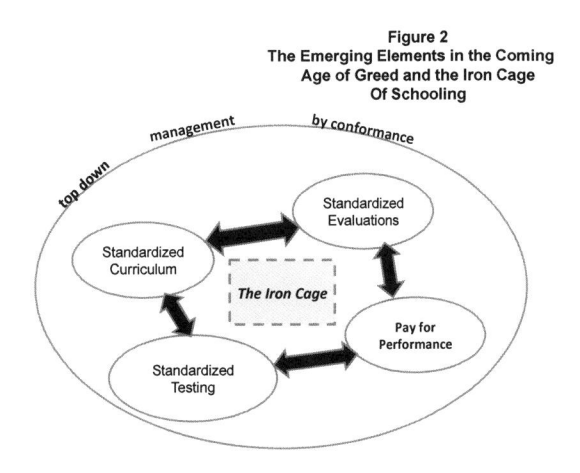

**Figure 2**
**The Emerging Elements in the Coming Age of Greed and the Iron Cage Of Schooling**

The first element is a standardized curriculum which amounts to a standardized plan of work. That is coming in the "Common Core" curriculum being pushed by the U.S. Department of Education and neoliberal think tanks as well as the Council of Chief State School Officers. A standardized plan of work permits standardized evaluations or work measurement now being developed by the Gates Foundation (see Gates & Gates, 2011). Part of the standardization of the work requires standardized outcome measures. That is provided by standardized tests whose structural content validity to the work itself is supplied by a standardized work plan (i.e., the "Common Core" curriculum). When that is in place now comes "performance pay" linked to evaluation, something that is now being legislated in nearly half the states (see Banchero, 2011d). All of these developments, in whole or in part, contribute to the construction of the *iron cage*.

The final ingredient of the *iron cage* is the installation of an authoritarian, top-down corporate model of *management by the numbers* to which salary and bonuses are then connected. This type of corporate management, called *managerialism* in the U.K. (Gunter, 1997), is the one used by school superintendents Rhee, Garcia, and Hall to name a few. It is the one right on the horizon and is the management model in the Obama Administration's *Race to the Top* and that advocated by Jeb Bush's Foundation for Excellence in Education and its offshoot group known as Chiefs for Change (Ujifusa, 2013).

Here is the profound shift in values embedded in the neoliberal changes pawned off as "reforms" for American education:

- The loss of the common school ideal and the sale of public space in the guise of voucher plans and charter schools which vitiate the concept of commonality at their core;
- The erasure of the ethic of public service to an ethic of self-interest (greed) as the major motivator for educational leadership;
- The loss of any humane vision for the purpose of education as a common good by helping humans become more human instead of saleable commodities in the contemporary work force as the sole measure of successful schooling;
- The technicization and de-professionalization of teaching and the advocacy of virulent union busting to downsize the teaching force and lower labor costs to maximize profits in privatized schooling;
- The de-professionalization of educational leadership preparation programs at the college and university levels in schools of education to advance the installation of management models based on marketization and a mindset anchored in profit making now dominate in business schools.

As Figure 2 shows, when all of the pieces are assembled, we will have arrived at the Weberian *iron cage*. This is the future as we turn the corner into the age of greed for educational leadership. It is a frightening prospect and it is to this issue I now turn.

# CONCLUSIONS: A STRATEGY FOR *REGRESSIONSVERBOT*

*The state as we know it—but perhaps we should talk in the past tense here— is a quite particular social world, whose official purpose is public service, service to the public and devotion to the general interest...It remains however that the official definition of state office—and of officials, who are mandated to serve, not serve themselves---is an extraordinary historical invention, an advance for humanity, in the same sense as art or science. The conquest is fragile, and always threatened with regression or disappearance. And it is all this that is now rejected as outmoded and belonging to a past era* (Bourdieu, 2008a, p.197).

We are witnessing an extraordinary, well-financed, determined group of corporate millionaires and billionaires that are financing a self-serving, destructive doctrine on school leaders and public education in America (Ravitch, 2010). And they have managed to find like-minded allies in the Obama administration including the President himself and Education Secretary Arne Duncan (Riley, 2009). Both praised the closing of Central Falls High School in Rhode Island where the principal and the teaching and support staffs were fired. What a tragedy that a Democratic administration has completely adopted the neoliberal, Republican educational agenda-- lock, stock and barrel (Kumashiro, 2008; Chennault, 2010; Richardson, 2011) including advancing millions of dollars to support neoliberal projects such as the KIPP schools, Teach for America, and charter schools in New Orleans (*Education Week*, 2013, p. 15) despite evidence that none have become the antidotes to the very problems that neoliberals have criticized the public schools for failing to fix (see Aronson, 2013; Baker and Ferris, 2011; Miron, 2010).

The National Education Policy Center at the University of Colorado gave the U.S. Department of Education its Bunkum Award in 2010, an award based on the noted meaningless, irrelevant and endless tirades of Congressman Felix Walker from Buncombe County in North Carolina in 1820. The Bunkum Award then stands for long-winded nonsense.

The NEPC's judges cited the U.S. Department of Education's *A Blueprint for Reform* for "...religiously avoided acknowledging or using the large body of high-quality research that the federal government itself had commissioned and published over the years. Second, they first raised our expectations with repeated assurances that are recommended policies would be solidly grounded in research—only to then dash those hopes in research summary after research summary" (National Education Policy Center, 2011a).

What is proposed here is a counter strategy described by Bourdieu (1998) called *Regressionsverbot*, a German word which means "a ban on backward movement with respect to social gains..." (p. 41). It means we must educate ourselves to the immensity of the challenge before us and take up the cause of resisting and fighting for democracy and keeping public education public. We must work to maintain public space for the public which is accountable to the public. American corporate leadership is profoundly anti-democratic. In the words of Lynn Stout (2007) writing in *The Wall Street Journal*:

*Successful corporations are not, and never have been, democratic institutions. Since the public corporation first evolved over a century ago, U.S. law has discouraged shareholders from taking an active role in corporate governance, and this 'hands off' approach has proven a recipe for tremendous success* (p. A17)

Alan Blinder (2012) a professor of economics and public affairs at Princeton University agreed when he said, "Not many successful companies are run as democracies; benign dictatorship works far better. All the checks and balances that characterize American democracy would drive a hard-charging CEO, accustomed to getting his own way, crazy" (p. A19).

One of the fundamental conflicts between corporate leadership and educational leadership is the matter of public accountability. The 'billionaire boys club' referred to by Diane Ravitch (2010) is not accountable to anyone but themselves. As Ravitch (2010) observes, "If voters don't like the foundations' reform agenda, they can't vote them out of office….They are bastions of unaccountable power" (p. 201). Stager (2008) also asks, "If schools become the playthings of a handful of billionaires, are they still public schools?" (p. 38).

In the end teaching is about telling the truth. It's about connecting the classroom to the best of humanity and its long journey from life as hand to mouth with only brief moments of respite from danger, disease, despotism and death. And it's about the rise and fall of civilizations. It's about heroes and villains. It's about ideals, greed, tyranny and disaster.

The teacher, every teacher, is but a bridge from the past to the present and into the future. It's about finding dignity every day. It's about hope because without hope no teacher can survive very long the trials and the times after lunch and recess when tired minds and young bodies do not want to bend to the discipline of finding the knowledge of which every society requires to remain a living and viable entity.

In those moments with only children, who are simultaneously innocent and acutely discerning of every foible and falsehood of the older generation, the teacher stands as if before a jury and is on trial not only as a truth teller, but as a representative of the best the society can offer its future citizens.

After a time in this daily struggle teachers can sell out and be sold out. Treating them as machines or as pawns while more powerful forces plot their future and strip them of the independence they bring to their calling, the hope they embody and are cherished for in every nation on earth, can be crushed. The day teachers give up caring about every child in their classrooms and care more about their bonuses for test scores is the day every civilization declines and is ultimately on its deathbed.

The neoliberal antidote to improving the schools ought to embolden and empower teachers to be successful. Instead, neoliberals propose an *iron cage*, a bureaucratic trap of tests and assessments, standardization, rewards and punishments embodied in top down control that crush the spirit and reduce their work to mindless drudgery and brain numbing accounting that trivialize their labors. Even Henry Ford, as hardened a business leader as there ever was, understood that he hired the whole person not just a pair of hands. He had to be concerned with the total human being.

Corporate leaders who have never been in a classroom day in and day out have no understanding of what Mahatma Gandhi, one of the most profound game changers in human history who was deeply skeptical of only reason and logic as his guide to action. Gandhi practiced *ahimsa* which was "a matter not of the intellect but of the heart" (Iyer,1973, p. 18). Corporate control is not only mindless it is heartless. No amount of money can buy optimism. No amount of money can make believers of the cynical. Money cannot buy faith in a future no one can specify.

The fundamental error neoliberals make in their so-called educational "reforms" is that their efforts robotize education. The irony is that in the name of freedom of the individual, they strip their teachers of that very freedom. The corporate agenda reduces the essential human variable to one that is minimally human and minimally variable (Argyris, 1972).

Corporate leaders just don't understand that while most classroom teachers work alone, teaching itself is a communal activity and as Dan Lortie (1969) observed, "The principle of *equality* is deeply rooted in the governance of American schools—a conception of equality as *sameness* pervades organizational life" (p. 7). It is an intricate web practitioners share comprised of common aspirations and norms.

However, teacher unions get it. The resiliency of teacher unions is centered on matters of teacher autonomy and freedom to be the masters of their own classrooms and work space. Corporate control will founder on this fundamental rock even if teacher unions did not exist because as Eric Hoffer (1951) wrote over a half-century ago, "Where freedom is real, equality is the passion of the masses. When equality is real, freedom is the passion of a small minority" (p.37).

Here is the essential rub. Teacher autonomy and freedom from administrative control is rooted in equality and their latitude to function independently is anchored there. Business leaders view equality with suspicion because their power and freedom is hierarchical, anti-democratic and deeply bureaucratic. Their freedom is therefore their ability to retain control and power by buying political influence and creating and gaining access to markets which then are privatized and profitized. A recent spate with Jeb Bush's Foundation for Excellence and Education and efforts to influence officials in Maine, Oklahoma and Rhode Island highlighted by the nonprofit group Public Interest in Washington, D.C. indicate that where equality is real in public space, freedom is important for a small minority in order to turn a profit (Ujifusa, 2013).

What neoliberals propose as their solution to the problems of education is authoritarian, top-down, corporate control, i.e., pure *managerialism,* oblivious to anything except the immediate profits to be made in market centric thinking and transactions. Chester Finn's (1991) book regarding what schools require to be better says it all, *We Must Take Charge* which is a typical corporate outlook of a manager in a machine bureaucracy (see Mintzberg, 1983, pp. 163-187).

Wolcott (1977) studied this problem over a quarter century ago in his book *Teachers vs. Technocrats* and wrote, "…teachers will most readily accept those changes that offer solutions to teacher problems. To use a homely metaphor, education's change agents have earned a reputation for 'scratching where it isn't itching'" (p. 245).

In this nexus educational leadership is both a problem and a solution to this dilemma. Leadership must call the neoliberals out and identify their agendas and self interests in what they propose as "reforms" (English, 2010; Ravitch 2005). Educational leadership must not only resist, but must be pugnacious and openly incredulous of neoliberal schemes, and if necessary even disrespectful, especially given neoliberal smugness about their own lack of reflexivity and their professed lack of self-interest in their schemes to make money in the name of "reform".

Neoliberals are pursuing an agenda which is a political ideology, that is, "those abstract (and rather dubious) theories allegedly based on reason or science, which tried to map out the social order and guide political action" (Boudon, 1989, p., 25).

We ought to be cognizant of Eric Hoffer's (1951) admonition, "The effectiveness of a doctrine does not come from the meaning but from its certitude. No doctrine however profound and sublime will be effective unless it is presented as the embodiment of the one and only truth. It must be the one word from which all things are and all things speak" (p. 76).

Any reading of neoliberal attacks on the public schools never reveal any doubt that their antidotes will work even when they don't and didn't (Bersin, 2005; Ravitch, 2010). A recent study on bonus pay conducted by Vanderbilt University showed that such a scheme "had no overall impact on student achievement" (Sawchuk, 2010, 1). Bonus pay is a pet remedy advanced by neoliberals to solve the problem of quality teaching (Bush, 2006; Fields, 2008; Gerstner, 2008). It just doesn't work (Sawchuk, 2012).

Educational leaders and the professors who prepare them must describe the damage neoliberal solutions will impose on the schools and ultimately on the society which depends upon them to graduate thoughtful, critical adults. Education is not only about math and science, but more importantly the crucible on which every civilization ultimately is judged, in the arts and humanities and what they offer to all peoples around the globe to become more fully human and humane.

Educational leadership must remain centered on the Latin word *educo* which means "to lead forth, draw out" (Andrews, 1854, p.515) instead of the concept "to pour in" knowledge as if pupils were empty buckets to be filled. The former term requires respect for difference and democracy (Woods, 2005), while the latter concept refers to autocratic domination and tight control to be sure what is poured in remains on tests (Finn, 1991; Jacobs 2010).

Chester E. Finn Jr. of the neoliberal think tank The Fordham Institute and Broad Foundation chooses to present two contrasts regarding how education professors see themselves in a recent report *Cracks in the Ivory Tower*. In a loaded dichotomy Finn says that education professors see themselves "as philosophers and agents of social change, not as master craftsmen sharing tradecraft" (Jacobs, 2010). Finn then extends this dichotomy as education professors believe that the proper role of the teacher is to be facilitator of learning instead of a conveyor of knowledge. This is definitely not *educo*. Finn laments that not as many education professors "believe it's as necessary for teachers to understand how to work with state standards, tests, and accountability systems" (Jacobs, 2010).

Clearly, Finn's neoliberal view is that teachers should knuckle under and accept their subservience as advanced by the neoliberal minions of top-down corporate control. Teachers need to become "tradesmen" and not professionals, and do what they are told as their future world is fashioned by neoliberal legislation. Education professors are therefore obstacles to preparing the "right" kind of teacher to fit into the current hierarchy of power as envisioned by neoliberal acolytes.

Ekman (2010) paused to consider the shifting nature of the types of individuals who were being named to higher education leadership positions. His concerns also deeply resonant with those for K-12 educational leadership roles:

>*...we should be concerned that a growing number of colleges are being led by people who have never had direct experience in the heart of the enterprise...if the number continue to increase, the risk is that higher education will become an industry that is led by people who do not truly understand it, who view it as a commodity to be traded, a production problem to be solved efficiently, or a brand to be marketed (p.A88).*

Similarly, Barry Glassner, President of Lewis & Clark College in Oregon also wrote that, "We doubt that any CEO, if asked to name his or her greatest challenge, would include on the list what we put near the top: the obligation to create civil communities in an era of incivility" (p. A56).

It is not too late to work to stem the neoliberal tide before it swamps our profession with the corrosive values of greed and corruption anchored in a for profit mindset that the only thing that matters is money and its acquisition, and what is "good" is to get even more money by skirting the rules or outright cheating. The data clearly show that when all that matters is money "...money crowds out norms" (Sandel,2012, p. 118). Those are the norms which pertain to social justice and to matters which continue to pull our social structure asunder and to exaggerate as oppose to resolve the achievement, attainment and opportunity gaps in American life.

Joseph Stiglitz (2012), the "other" American winner of the Nobel Prize in Economics (besides Milton Friedman) observed:

>*We can judge our system by its results, and if we do so, we have to give it a failing grade: a little while ago those at the bottom and in the middle got a glimpse of the American dream, but today's reality is that for a large segment of the population that dream has now vanished ( p.274).*

The social consequences of abandoning the idea of the American common school, which is about to slip into the dustbin of educational history, will be the continuation and extension of the huge wealth disparities which threaten the very well being of America (Irvin, 2008; Wilkinson & Pickett, 2010; Stiglitz 2012). Neoliberal think tanks are now even running charter schools (Robelen, 2006).

If the schools are re-grounded from the engine of equality and social justice to the reinforcement of wealth, privilege and the existing form of political power which insures they remain the same (Spring 1989), the American dream will also be gone forever (see Bratlinger, 2003). The public schools will only be public for the children who have no where else to go and accepted there because no one else wants them.

There is already evidence that EMOs and charter schools consistently under enroll special needs students (Miron & Nelson, 2002; Banchero & Porter, 2012) which has led to "the restratification and isolation of students by race, class, special education status, and English language learner status...Further, 43 percent of black charter school students attended schools that were 99 percent minority. By contrast, less than 15 percent of black students in traditional public schools attend such highly segregated schools" (Mead & Green, 2012).

There is however, some cause for optimism for as Pierre Bourdieu (1999b) has reminded us that, "…what the social world has done, it can, armed with this knowledge, undo. In any event what is certain is that nothing is less innocent than noninterference" (p. 629). Bourdieu was insistent that we must use "fully the margin of maneuver left to liberty, that is, to political action" (p. 629). While public school classroom teachers may choose a form of political activism that involves refusing to give standardized tests as they have in Seattle, Washington recently (Banchero, 2013), professors have a different avenue of political action available to them. It is to this matter I now turn.

# PURSUING PUSHBACK TO CORPORATE REFORM

At the end of the film *The Wizard of Oz*, the heroine, Dorothy, discovers that Oz is just a man and despite being told by him, "Don't pay any attention to the man behind the curtain," she recognizes him for what he is—an imposter. Neoliberal "reformers" are imposters. And that is where they can be successfully fought.

Gene V. Glass, a long time respected researcher in our field, observed that, "The corporations just woke up a few years ago to the billions and billions of dollars that exist in public education, and they just decided to go for it. The incredible thing is how easy it is" (Davis, 2013, p. 52).

Neoliberalism is an ideology and not a scientific theory. Because it isn't a scientific theory it can't be researched *as a theory* because it isn't true or false. Rather, neoliberalism is a socio-economic-political ideology which poses itself as something for the common good, but is anything but common and good only for a few. It is an imposter which uses the language of democracy to preserve the privilege of the few. Neoliberal advocates put out the expected outcomes of neoliberal, market driven solutions to education. When they don't pan out, they argue that they were not implemented with either fidelity or sufficient motivation. True believers never doubt their own beliefs.

Neoliberal advocates and adherents have cleverly learned to use the language of change they desire as "reform" to mask their own self-interests in that pursuit. Academics are listening to the wrong language in confronting neoliberal attacks. Academics pursue debate as though all parties are interested in knowing the truth about things. Neoliberals have no such qualms. They are *not interested* in the truth. They *are* interested in making money. Neoliberals are *not interested* in *civil service*. They are interested in *civil privatism* (McCarthy, 1989, p. 369).

Most academics I know are truth seekers. Most academics in the schools of education I know believe in the virtue of the common good. They believe in social justice. They see the schools as vital to the security of the nation and the promise of that nation reaching the highest ideals for *all*. It isn't "make as much money as you can" but rather "we need to be as good as we can". And good means for "everybody." And it's not something that can be bought and sold because it isn't for sale.

Civic virtue, the value of an ethic of public service in the name of the public is not dead. The last time I saw a list of who the public trusts the most, at the top of the list were our military service personnel and medical doctors, with teachers being somewhere in the middle (see Rice, 2011). Near the bottom were business leaders and bankers.

The general public does understand honesty. They do "get" corruption and how it eats away at providing good public services for everyone's improved quality of life, whether in medicine, the environment or in education. The general public does understand self-interest. This is the big stick the neoliberals have used to beat up teachers' unions by claiming they are more interested in serving adults than children (Klein, 2012).

The fabricated image is thus drawn that only selfish, mediocre and bad teachers belong to unions. That thousands of "good" teachers also belong to unions is somehow never mentioned in editorials in the *Wall Street Journal*. That many of the so-called "reforms" being pushed by neoliberal advocates demean, demonize, and de-professionalize teachers are rarely if ever considered. All opposition is cast as obstructionist and self-serving. How teachers are supposed to continue to provide a good service to all children, no matter who they are or where they are as they are being systematically denigrated, is a contradiction that begs for explanation, but is rarely pursued with much interest by corporate foundation funders (Weingarten, 2011).

And what is ironic and left unsaid is how the "reforms" will benefit the reformers. They don't talk about that in public, but we must talk about that in public. We must point out to the public whose pockets are being lined when neoliberals advocate "educational reform" (Davis, 2013). We must be clear about who is benefitting from the implementation of their agenda and who is not:

- The real agenda is not about improving test scores, but selling more tests;
- The real agenda is not about improving curricular rigor, but about standardizing curriculum in order to sell more books, materials, and computers to implement that curriculum;
- The real agenda is not about improving teaching and the life of teachers, but simplifying teaching with standardized evaluations, thus reducing the need for specialization and expertise and with it overall labor costs;
- The real agenda is not to improve public education, but to sell it to the highest bidder in the form of vouchers and charter schools and to create markets for EMOs to penetrate, profitize and proliferate;
- The real agenda is not to equalize learning, thus reducing the achievement gap, but to permit the extension of the gap by erasing the need to have outstanding schools for all children under the guise of choice to rationalize our collective failure to effectively educate children of the poor.

The neoliberal assault on leadership preparation in schools of education is masked in the language of business efficiency, a tactic with a long and tawdry history in educational administration (Callahan, 1960). The real agenda of the neoliberals is to replace a mindset which is founded on service for the common good, the dominant and pervasive perspective in most university based educational leadership programs, with a mindset founded on the *for-profit* monetary definition of success found in most business schools.

Neoliberals understand that to implement their market based ideology with all of the attendant concepts regarding money and profit, they must replace the dominant public service perspective with one that is primarily motivated by marketized rewards. They must remake education into a business (Cuban, 2004).

To enable the *for profit* approach to be successful in education requires privatization and ruthless standardization in order to optimize financial return. That is what is really behind the proposal to replace the Ed.D. with the MBA (Levine, 2005; Maranto, Ritter & Levine, 2010).

Educational leadership programs at colleges and universities have been singled out as the major culprits for neoliberal "reforms" not being tried because their graduates don't come to their positions with a primary value orientation centered in their own self-interest and the prospect of their next bonus check for standardized test score gains.

The "bottom line" is that neoliberal educational "reform" can't prevail without being anchored in greed. The corruption that inevitably accompanies that outlook is the public agenda where our pushback work lies. We can begin this undertaking by knowing that there is a deep appreciation by the public about what constitutes corruption which has been provided in sordid detail by the world of business and banking which continues unabated.

The loss of public confidence in corporate America has been profound. Public skepticism anchored in the concept of fairness within the "background justice" that John Rawls (2003) describes is real, alive and tangible. The outrage from some of the Federal Court judges in adjudicating the most egregious examples of greed in the corporate world is but a reflection of the general public's outrage. We must build on this reservoir as the legacy of our labors to keep American public education public and to stop and reverse the culture of corruption that threatens to engulf us. When we speak out we will find that we are not alone. That is our work. That is our calling. It is our version of our own *heritage foundation*.

# EPILOGUE
*Reclaiming Public Education*

*Carol A. Mullen*

*Educational Leadership in the Age of Greed: A Requiem for Res Publica* is a manifesto that critiques educational policy and politics in an engaging scholarly way. I see it as a powerful articulation in support of a public intellectual's grassroots "defense of research, education, and action for the public good" (ReclaimAERA, 2013). Prolific author Dr. Fenwick English, distinguished professor of educational leadership at The University of North Carolina at Chapel Hill and former president of the National Council of Professors of Educational Administration (NCPEA), is a strong defender of the mission of public schools, the principled education of all children and youth, and the capacity of teachers and administrators to be accountable to their communities as socially just advocates.

This book offers wisdom to all who truly care about this mission and to the younger generation that is seeking to be educated, heart and mind. The elders in our academic village grew up in a different time when a common school was the context in which we were socialized to be human and humane. I believe that we must take it upon ourselves to understand the thoughtful and provocative argument proffered in this book about the current times described as the age of greed. Readers will gain from having a more complete understanding of how neoliberalism—not a smooth, well-oiled machine that one can easily point a finger at but rather a mechanistic force consisting of many moving parts across corporate structures and within educational systems—works in and against our schools and in and against our work as leaders, teachers, and citizens.

Just before I read *Educational Leadership in the Age of Greed*, I had attended the American Educational Research Association (AERA) convention in San Francisco, ready to do my usual gig of giving presentations, performing as a discussant, and attending sessions and business meetings on social justice leadership. However, this scenario changed when all around me AERA attendees were speaking in whispers. "Not in my name" was a provocative sign held up by many protesters during a speech that US Secretary of Education Arne Duncan gave.

Present at this main event in May 2013 in a banquet room stuffed with hundreds of educators from around the world, the "not in my name" sign was a prominent one that protested AERA's invitation to Duncan to speak. Checking with my international colleagues also in attendance, we read the sign as meaning that the protesters were not in agreement with the US government's testing policies. Anti-testing fliers were being circulated and picketers had displayed other anti neoliberal messages such as "charter schools cheery pick students and "Yes to respect!," presumably on behalf of public school teachers and students (ReclaimAERA, 2013).

When I read Dr. English's book, it brought to mind some important "signs" that were missing on that day of public protest, such as "educators against greed" and "take back our schools, now!" These signs or messages that I am imaginatively construing and those actually carried on that day of protest would likely be conceptualized as a desirable level of action in English's manifesto. As a pedagogue, I discussed these observations over dinner with two of my doctoral students, seated principals who toil daily on behalf of children living in poverty. When I asked them "what sign would you write and carry around if you could?" one said "sacrificial lamb" and the other responded "tired of the game." Our social justice advocates who are fighting the fight feel "damn worn out" to quote them precisely. But like Dr. English I think that if we are really lucky and band together it may not be too late to reclaim public education for the betterment of our school communities and for the health of our nation states.

I am inviting you to learn from sharing your reactions about this book with your own constituent groups, whether they be teachers you are preparing for careers in schools, prospective administrative leaders, seated central district personnel, or another group. Just by taking one small step like this, or holding up (or deciding on) your own sign of protest, we can all be productively contributing to the grassroots movement afoot in education that protests corporate greed and the ruin of public schools. We the people who take thoughtful action, especially as a force in our own name, will be exposing the "underbelly" (hidden realities and untruths of neoliberal ideology) of the "shark" (neoliberalism and the attack on public education). One by one and united we can put a stop to the bloodletting—those actions taken by leeches that are destroying public education values. It is not always easy to identify who or what they are, even though Dr. English connects some of the dots for us, partly by revealing who is attached to what monetary gains within school systems. Education is big business in America. As he attests, conservative marketers are politically savvy—they resort to magic tricks and lexical games by using the same language as supporters of public education. Freedom. Liberation. Deregulation. Choice. America.

While it is revolutionary these days for hundreds of educators to band together to speak out against the dismantling of public education by marketers and public policy figures representing public institutions, it is sobering to recognize that even speaking out can be silencing. On that day of protest at AERA there was simultaneously suppression of free speech and robust intellectual dialogue. Free speech ironically took the non-verbal form of signs, arm bands, fliers, and protest lines. Protesters gathered and generated momentum behind the scenes and outside the banquet room where Arnie Duncan spoke into a microphone. Double speak—not thoughtful point and counter point as is customary in rigorous intellectual debate—was reflected in rhetoric that was both for and against test-based accountability. After conceding that there are some problems with standardized tests, Duncan underscored the need for better tests!

The educational community may finally be ready to hear Dr. English's bold and assertive message to (1) reclaim public education as a common school that allows for criticality and equity to be fostered as core values of education, and (2) defend it against neoliberal assaults that treat public education as a consumable commodity that can be traded, bought, and sold. Many readers will not be surprised by the courageous public stand Dr. English takes against the corporatization, standardization, and privatization of education. With this book, he persists in protesting the neoliberal message and unapologetically naming those influential conservatives such as Arne Duncan who represent and support it. He explains technocratic, dehumanizing forces of privatization and takes them apart with his bare hands to show us how they work.

Education as a public service must be kept alive and cherished. This core value permeates the book. After reading *Educational Leadership in the Age of Greed*, educators from public institutions should feel better equipped to re-engage in the liberation of education as a public good. We are also being called upon to work against the narrowing of possibilities of what it means to research, know, learn, and communicate our understandings and counter the marginalizing and silencing of voices of dissent (see ReclaimAERA, 2013). What forces do you think are destroying institutions and educational values, forging divisions across society that includes labor and social relations? Explaining these complex phenomena from the perspective of your own position and life, what would you say and what examples would you give?

Dr. English points to the insidious blood flow of neoliberalism in our daily lives and the news we read. For example, think about how the amount of testing proposed by the US Department of Education in connection to national standards is increasing. Testing has become excessive to the point of including all subjects that can be tested and more grade levels. Think about how "interim" tests will be given and maybe pretests to measure growth, defined as increases in standardized test scores or "value-added" measures. Now think about the financial cost of implementing standards and electronically delivering national tests. To offset the enormous costs, funding will be bled from school activities that promote learning and from the arts and humanities. As English, Papa, Mullen, and Creighton (2012) have argued, advocacy has a focus and it is poverty: This money could be spent to ameliorate the effects of poverty, such as meal programs, medical staff, and libraries, especially for children living in the most poverty-stricken areas.

As this book's core message for educational leadership and leaders makes clear, we must assess the damage neoliberal solutions (such as more testing and more funding for more testing) will impose on the schools. What values will our children grow up to have? These days, they are getting the message that education is about math and science and being globally competitive. As Dr. English eloquently writes about elsewhere (see English, 2008), the possibilities that the arts and humanities hold for people is to become more fully human and humane as fully engaged citizens.

NCPEA Living Legend English's passionate, explicitly political plea advocates for a public education that serves all children, everywhere, and against capitalist greed that feeds on children instead of helping to feed them. He presents this vision for transformational leadership as a fundamental part of what former school superintendent and executive director of the American Association of School Administrators Paul Houston (2006) describes as "the spirit of the commonwealth that has always been the central expectation of public education" (p. 5).

*Educational Leadership in the Age of Greed* is a gripping tribute to humanity while also being a work of resistance on behalf of leaders who must work to promote the common good and what English refers to as "education as a public service for the public" (p. 1). This book makes urgency palatable. Push back is the necessary agency for resisting being overtaken and fed upon, tricked even!, by for-profit educators and educational reforms that bloodlet schools, families, and communities. Even poverty can be fed upon. This outrage must be stopped.

On a larger scale of social resistance, this book proffers a powerful critique of the neoliberal trend that bloodlets at a proliferating pace in public education and in a myriad of forms that include but extend well beyond charter schools, vouchers, and corporate branding. While bloodletting refers to the removal of blood, usually from a vein, as a therapeutic measure, this is how bad things (like high-stakes testing and tenure elimination) are made to look good; bloodletting also refers to the laying off of personnel and the elimination of resources (*The Free Dictionary*, 2013).

In all of these respects and more, English takes on the neoliberal movement, exposing each of these capitalist elements that belong to "the shark," revealing the neoliberal enterprise for what it really is (not for what it is made to look like). While my commentary on English's argument uses metaphors of shark and bloodletting, he uses metaphors of iron cage and switchmen. He provides background on the scientific management paradigm and unravels the inner workings of machine bureaucracy, particularly concerning matters of control, conformity, and standardization in the current policy era and political arena. This pithy book can be read by study groups or even alone during work breaks. I encourage you to mull over the ideas.

Why? English's work of intellectual vigor stands alongside manifestos that profoundly critique antidemocratic trends, perhaps namely Bourdieu's (1998) *Acts of Resistance* and Giroux's (2004) *The Terror of Neoliberalism*. English affirms and builds upon these books in his own argument. Since Giroux's book on neoliberalism appeared 10 years ago, the high-stakes testing culture in American has gotten much worse—inequities and poverty are on the rise and threats against education and schools are more forceful, personally and professionally intimidating (English et al, 2012).

*Educational Leadership in the Age of Greed*, an important and timely book by one of our leading intellectuals in education and educational leadership more specifically, challenges us to rethink the dominant political wisdom and our own responsibility for countering the for-profit, anti-intellectual mindset that hurts schools, teachers, and students and for transforming education into that which honors the public school mission. English's wake-up call concerning the destruction of the idea and practice of public service puts current federal legislation under a microscope, along with the latest neoliberal takeovers of schools. He draws our attention to the sneak attacks that implicate innocent children and that subvert their authentic learning. The neoliberal infestation in the world of higher education is also animated; regarding the preparation of teachers and leaders, he discusses managerialism in the teaching and preparation of future leaders and pedagogues for schools and presents this as a technology, really a neoliberal maneuver to take over schools and their future through the preparation of school leaders. In his critique, programs and people, ideas and language are being commodified, that is, marketed, measured, and packaged. As collective values fade, English attests, the new corporate state distances itself from workers and ethnic minority groups that become disposable and that live with manufactured fear.

The legacy of this book is its depiction of the shark-like grip of conservative forces and for-profit agendas and the children of poverty and struggling schools that need to be released from this grip—in English's terminology, the iron cage of control. The swift takeover of American public education by neoliberal ideology and think tanks that have dwarfed public education as we once knew it presents one level of understanding. The way that English takes us into this underworld exposes the shark for what it really is. The spirit of public service needs to survive—education for the common good is good for all children.

# REFERENCES

Adams, R & Vascellaro, J. (2010, December 13). News Corp. draws study plan. *The Wall Street Journal.*

Anderson, G. L. & Pini, M. (2011). Educational leadership and the new economy: Keeping the 'public' in the public schools. In F.W. English (Ed.) *The Sage handbook of educational leadership*, 2nd Ed (pp.176-222). Thousand Oaks: Sage.

Andrews, E.A. (1854). *Copious and critical Latin-English lexicon.* New York: Harper & Brothers Publishers, p.515.

Anonymous (2011, July 15). The fear and frustration of faculty at for-profit colleges. *The Chronicle Review,* B12-B13.

Apple, M. (2006). *Educating the "Right" way: Markets, standards, God, and inequality, 2nd ed.* New York: Routledge.

Argyris, C. (1972). *The applicability of organizational sociology.* London, UK: Cambridge University Press.

Aronson, L.B. (2013, April 24). Advice to TFA from a former insider. *Education Week,* 32 (29), 24.

Baker, B. & Ferris, R. (2011). Adding up the spending: Fiscal disparities and philanthropy among New York City charter schools. National Education Policy Center. Retrieved at http://nepc.colorado.edu/publication/NYC-charter.disparities on January 27 2011.

Banchero, S. (2010, July 24). Teachers lose jobs over test scores. *The Wall Street Journal,* A3.

Banchero, S. (2011a, January 4). Illinois attempts to link teacher tenure to results. *The Wall Street Journal,* A3.

Banchero, S. (2011b, January 11). School changes pushed by group. *The Wall Street Journal,* A7.

Banchero, S. (2011c, July 16). Hundreds of teachers are dismissed in Washington for poor performance. *The Wall Street Journal,* A3.

Banchero, S. (2011d, October 26). Nearly half the states link teacher evaluations to tests. *The Wall Street Journal,* A5.

Banchero, S. (2013, January 26-27). Seattle teachers protest exams. *The Wall Street Journal,* A3.

Banchero, S. & Porter, C. (2012, June 20). Fewer disabled go to charter schools. *The Wall Street Journal,* A2.

Banchero, S. & McWhirter, C. (2013, April 13-14). Efforts to curb cheating bog down. *The Wall Street Journal,* A6.

Banjo, S. (2012, April 2). Wal-Mart to pay $4.8 million in back wages, damages. *The Wall Street Journal,* B3.

Bankston, C.L. & Caldas, S.J. (2009). *Public education—America's civil religion.* New York: Teacher's College Press.

Barry, B. (2005). *Why social justice matters.* Cambridge, UK: Polity Press.

Belkin, D. (2012, July 3). For-profit colleges score a victory. *The Wall Street Journal,* A3.

Berrett, D. (2013, May 3). 2 years of for-profit college? Earnings no better than after high school. *The Chronicle of Higher Education,* 59 (34), A17.

Bersin, A.D.(2005, April 20). The point of accountability and the key to renewal. *Education Week*, 24 (32), 40.

Blau, P.M. & Scott, W.R. (1962). *Formal organizations: A comparative approach.* San Francisco, CA: Chandler Publishing Company.

Blinder, A. S. (2012, October 2). The case against a CEO in the oval office. *The Wall Street Journal*, A19.

Blumenstyk, G. (2004, October 8). U. of Phoenix uses pressure in recruiting, report says. *The Chronicle of Higher Education*, 51 (7), A1-A27.

Blumenstyk, G. (2012, March 9). For-profit colleges compute their own graduation rates. *The Chronicle of Higher Education*, 58 (27), A14.

Blumenstyk, G. (2011, April 8). Colleges scramble to avoid violating federal-aid limit. *The Chronicle of Higher Education*, 57 (31). A1, A6.

Blumenstyk, G. & Richards, A. (2011, March 18). For-profit colleges manage defaults to mask problems, analysis indicates. *The Chronicle of Higher Education*, 57 (28). A1, A6.

Bolton, C. L. & English, F.W. (2010). De-constructing the logic/emotion binary in educational leadership preparation and practice. *Journal of Educational Administration*, 48 (5), 561-578.

Borg, W.R. & Gall, M.D. (1989). *Educational research: An introduction, 5th Ed.* New York: Longman.

Borja, R.R.(2006, October 12). Bennett quits K12, Inc. under fire. *Education Week*, 25 (7), 6.

Borja, R.R. (2004, September 29). *Education Week,* 24 (5) 8.

Boudon, R. (1989). *The analysis of ideology.* M. Slater, Trans. Chicago: The University of Chicago Press.

Bouie, J.(2013, May 24). Not how DeMint planned it. *The Week,* 13, (618), 12.

Bourdieu, P. (1991). *Language and symbolic power.* Cambridge, MA: Harvard University Press.

Bourdieu, P. (1998). *Acts of resistance: Against the tyranny of the market, In R. Nice, Trans.* New York: The New Press.

Bourdieu, P. (1999a). The abdication of the state. In P. Bourdieu, et. al. (Eds) *The weight of the world: Social suffering in contemporary society*. P.P. Ferguson, et. al. Trans.(pp. 181-188). Stanford, CA: Stanford University Press.

Bourdieu, P. (1999b). Postscript. In P. Bourdieu, et. al. (Eds.). *The weight of the world: Social suffering in contemporary society*. P.P. Ferguson, et. al. Trans. (pp. 627-629). Stanford, CA: Stanford University Press.

Bourdieu, P. (2001). *Firing back: Against the tyranny of the market 2,* L. Wacquant, Trans. New York: The New Press.

Bourdieu, P. (2008a). Our wretched state. In P. Bourdieu (Ed.) *Political interventions: Social science and political action* (pp. 197-204). London: Verso.

Bourdieu, P. (2008b). *Outline of a theory of practice.* Cambridge, UK: Cambridge University Press.

Boyle, P. & Burns, D. (2012). *Preserving the public in public schools: Visions, values, conflict and choices.* Lanham, MD: Rowman & Littlefield Publishers.

Brantlinger, E. (2003). *Dividing classes: How the middle class negotiates and rationalizes school advantage.* New York: RoutledgeFalmer.

Bray, C.(2013a, March 29). SAC deal to settle charges on hold. *The Wall Street Journal,* C1.

Bray, C. (2013b, May 3). Former fund manager is sentenced. *The Wall Street Journal,* C2.

Bray, C. (2013c, May 14). Fund co-founder sentenced in insider case. *The Wall Street Journal,* C3.

Bray, C. (2012, October 19). Three sentenced in bid-rigging case. *The Wall Street Journal,* C3.

Bray, C. & Baer, J. (2013, April 4). Ex-trader admits to fraud. *The Wall Street Journal,* C3.

Broad, E. (2012, May 23). Never let a crisis go to waste. *Education Week,* 31 (32). 28.

Broad Foundation (2001). Retrieved from http://broadeducation.org/news/137.html

Broad Foundation (2013a). Retrieved from http://www.broadcenter.org/academy/network/resources

Broad Foundation (2013b). Retrieved from http://www.broadcenter.org/academy/about

Broad Foundation (2013c). Retrieved from http://broadcenter.org/how-bureaucracy-stands-in-the-way

Brock, D. (2004). *The republican noise machine: Right-wing media and how it corrupts democracy.* New York: Three Rivers Press.

Burd, S. (2004, July 30). Selling out higher-education policy? *The Chronicle of Higher Education,* 50 (47), A16.

Burns, J.M. (1978). *Leadership.* New York: Harper & Row.

Bush, J. (2006, January 30). Five rules for school reform. *The Wall Street Journal,* A19.

Bush, J. & Klein, J. (2011, June 24). The case for common educational standards. *The Wall Street Journal,* A13.

Callahan, D. (2004). *The cheating culture.* Orlando, FLA: Harcourt, Inc.

Callahan, R.E. (1960). *Education and the cult of efficiency.* Chicago: University of Chicago Press.

Carnoy, M., Jacobsen, R., Mishel, L. & Rothstein, R. (2005). *The charter school dust-up: Examining the evidence on enrollment and achievement.* Washington, D.C. The Economic Policy Institute and Teachers College Press.

Chennault, R. (2010, May 19). Obama-Era education policy. *Education Week,* 29 (32), 30-31.

*Chronicle of Higher Education* (2004, October 8). For-profit colleges under scrutiny. 51 (7), A29.

*Chronicle of Higher Education* (2004, October 8). For-profit colleges under scrutiny. 51 (7), A29.

*Chronicle of Higher Education* (2005, November 11). The Chronicle index of for-profit higher education A31.

*Chronicle of Higher Education* (2011a, March 18). For-profit colleges manage defaults to mask problems, analysis indicates. 57 (28), A1.

*Chronicle of Higher Education* (2011b, May 13). Faculty as pawns? 57 (36), A10.

Clark, D. (2012, December 12). A record patent verdict. *The Wall Street Journal,* B1.

Colchester, M. & Passariello, C. (2011, December 8). Dirty secrets in soap prices. *The Wall Street Journal,* B2.

Conason, J. (2003). *Big lies: The right-wing propaganda machine and how it distorts the truth.* New York: Thomas Dunne Books.

Condron, D.J. (2011). Egalitarianism and educational excellence: Compatible goals for affluent societies. *Educational Researcher,* 40 (2), 47-55.

Cools, K. (2005, March 22). Ebbers Rex. *The Wall Street Journal*, B2.

Critchley, S. (1992). *The ethics of deconstruction.* Oxford, England: Blackwell.

Cuban, L. (2004). *The blackboard and the bottom line*: *Why schools can't be businesses.* Cambridge, MA: Harvard University Press.

Davis, M.R. (2013, April 24). Education industry players exert public-policy influence. *Education Week,* 32 (29), 52-53.

De Vise, D. (2010, August 4). Fraud found in college recruiting. *The Washington Post*, A2.

*Economist* (2012, July 21). Free exchange. Fine and punishment. 404 (8794). 64.

*Education Week* (2013, June 5). A look under the hood. 32 (33), 15.

Edwards, L. (2013, May 13). A heritage of liberty. *The Wall Street Journal*, A13.

Ehrich, L.C. & English, F.W. (2012). What can grassroots leadership teach us about school leadership? *Halduskultuur-Administrative Culture, 13* (2), 85-108.

Ekman, R. (2010, September 24). The imminent crisis in college leadership. *The Chronicle of Higher Education*, 57 (5), A88.

Emery, K., & Ohanian, S. (2004). *Why is corporate America bashing our public schools?* Portsmouth, NH: Heinemann.

English, F., (2000). A Critical Interrogation of Murphy's Call for a New Center of Gravity in In Educational Administration, *Journal of School Leadership* (September, 2000) 10 (5), 445-463.

English, F. (2003). Cookie-Cutter Leaders for Cookie-Cutter Schools: The Teleology of Standardization and the De-Legitimization of the University in Educational Leadership Preparation. *Leadership and Policy in Schools, 2*(1), 27-46.

English, F.W. (2004). Learning 'Manifestospeak': A metadiscursive analysis of the Fordham Institute's and Broad Foundation's Manifesto for Better Leaders for America's Schools. In T. Lasley (Ed.) *Better leaders for America's schools: Perspectives on the Manifesto* (pp. 52-91). Columbia, MO: University Council for Educational Administration.

English, F. W. (2008). *Art of educational leadership: Balancing performance and accountability.* Thousand Oaks, CA: Sage.

English, F.W. (2010, October). The ten most wanted enemies of American public education's school leadership. *NCPEA's Education Leadership Review,* 11 (2), 59-72.

English, F.W. (2011). Caveat emptor: Buyer beware of some inter-agency and non-profit collaboration with neoliberal foundations and think tanks. Paper presented at the National Council of Professors of Educational Administration Summer Conference, Portland, Oregon.

English, F.W. (2012, May). Bourdieu's *misrecognition:* why educational leadership standards will not reform schools or leadership. *Journal of Educational Administration and History,* 44 (2), 155-170.

English, F.W. (2013). Postmodernism: The Anti-Theory" in B. Irby, G. Brown, R. Lara-Alecio and S. Jackson (Eds.). *The handbook of educational theories* (pp. 871-876). Charlotte, NC. Information Age Publishing.

English, F. W., Papa, R., Mullen, C. A., & Creighton, T. (2012). *Educational leadership at 2050: Conjectures, challenges and promises.* Lanham, MD: Rowman & Littlefield Education.

English, F.W. & Crowder, Z. (2013). Counterspin: A discourse analysis of Eli Broad's leadership brag sheet. Symposium paper given at the American Educational Research Association, San Francisco, California, on May 1.

Enrich, D., Patrick, M. & Colchester, M. (2013, April 4). Report cites Barclays failings . *The Wall Street Journal,* C3.

Enrich, D. & Eaglesham, J. (2012, December 20). UBS admits rigging rates in epic plot. *The Wall Street Journal,* A1, A14.

Fairclough, N. (1992). *Discourse and social change.* London: Polity Press.

Feith, D. (2012, February 25-26). Triggering school reform—and union dirty tricks. *The Wall Street Journal*, A11.

Feith, D. (2012, September 15-16). Rahmbo at the school barricades. *The Wall Street Journal*, A11.

Field, K. (2010, September 10). For-profits spend heavily to fend off new rule. *The Chronicle of Higher Education*, 57 (3), A1, A16.

Field, K. (2011a, March 11). Senators consider plan to reduce federal payouts to for-profit colleges. *The Chronicle of Higher Education*, 57 (27), A23.

Field, K. (2011b, May 13). Faculty at for-profits allege constant pressure to keep students enrolled. *The Chronicle of Higher Education*, 57 (36), A1, A10.

Fields, G. (2008, November 11). D.C. schools chief scores gains, ruffles feathers. *The Wall Street Journal*, A6.

*Financial Times* (2012, December 17). Banks must learn from past scandals. 8.

Finn, C.E. Jr. (1991). *We Must Take Charge.* New York: Basic Books, Inc.

Finn, C.E. Jr. (2010, December 8). A sputnik moment for U.S. education. *The Wall Street Journal*, A21.

*Free Dictionary, The.* (2013). Retrieved from http://www.thefreedictionary.com/bloodletting.

Friedman, M. (1962). *Capitalism and freedom.* Chicago: University of Chicago Press.

Friere, P. (1970). *Pedagogy of the oppressed.* M. Ramos, Trans. New York: Seabury Press.

Feulner, E.J. & Needham, M.A. (2010, April 12). New fangs for the conservative 'beast'. *The Wall Street Journal*, A19.

Forelle, C. (2002, October 22). Flunked by investors, Edison schools scorns talk of failure. *The Wall Street Journal*, B1.

*Free Dictionary, The.* (2013). Retrieved from http://www.thefreedictionary.com/bloodletting.

Gates, B. & Gates, M. (2011, October 22-23). Grading the teachers. *The Wall Street Journal*, C3.

Gee, J.P. (1999). *An introduction to discourse analysis. Theory and practice.* New York, NY: Routledge.

Gerstner, L.V. Jr. (2008, December 1). Lessons from 40 years of education 'reform' *The Wall Street Journal,* A23.

Gillum, J. & Bello, M. (2011, March 30). When standardized test scores soared in D.C., were the gains real? *USA Today. Retrieved* at http://www. Usatoday.com/news/education on March 28, 2011.

Giroux, H.A. (2004). *The terror of neoliberalism: Authoritarianism and the eclipse of democracy.* Boulder, CA: Paradigm Publishers.

Glassner, B. (2013, February 15). College presidents: Bruised, battered, and loving it. *The Chronicle of Higher Education,* 59 (23), A56.

Greenfield, T.B. (1975). Theory about organization: A new perspective and its implications for schools. In M. G. Hughes (Ed.), *Administering education: International challenge* (pp. 71-99). London: Athlone.

Grunberg, S. & Moen, A.A.(2011, March 30). Nokia assails Apple again with new patent complaint. *The Wall Street Journal,* B6.

Gunter, H. (1997). *Rethinking education: The consequences of Jurassic management.* London, UK: Cassell.

Hacker, J.S. & Piersen, P. (2010). *Winner-take-all politics: How Washington made the rich richer—and turned its back on the middle class.* New York: Simon & Schuster.

Halliday, M.A.K. (1978). *Language as social semiotic.* London: Edward Arnold.

Hanushek, E.A. (2010, October 19). There is no 'war on teachers'. *The Wall Street Journal*, A-17.

Harvey, D. (2005). *A brief history of neoliberalism.* Oxford, UK: Oxford University Press.

Hechinger, J. & Sataline, S. (2009, March 12). For more mayors, school takeovers are a no-brainer. *The Wall Street Journal*, A12.

Hernstein, R.J. & Murray C. (1994). *The bell curve: Intelligence and class structure in American life.* New York: The Free Press.

Henninger, D. (2012, December 8-9). A lesson in conservative optimism. *The Wall Street Journal*, A15.

Hess, F.W. (2003a, January 8). What is 'public' about public education? *Education Week,* 22 (16), 56.

Hess, F.M. (2003b, July 9). A license to lead? *Education Week,* 22 (42)., 39.

Hess, F.M. (2012, December 18). The irrational fear of for-profit education. *The Wall Street Journal*, A-15.

Hinojosa, A. (2013, April 25). Ousted EPISD principal Luis Loya gives up fight, resigns. Retrieved at Google: *El Paso Times,* Paso School Scandal on June 13, 2013.

Hoffer, E. (1951). *The true believer: Thoughts on the nature of mass movements.* New York: Harper & Row.

Houston, P. (2006). The superintendent: Championing the deepest purposes of education. In P. Kelleher & R. Van Der Bogert (Eds.), *Voices for democracy: Struggles and celebrations of transformational leaders* (p. 109). Yearbook of the National Society for the Study of Education. Malden, MA: Blackwell.

Irvin, G. (2008). *Super rich: The rise of inequality in Britain and the United States.* Malden, MA: The Polity Press.

Iyer, R.N. (1973). *The moral and political thought of Mahatma Gandhi.* New York: Oxford University Press.

Jacobs, J. (2010, September 29). Education profs don't teach tradecraft. Retrieved from http://www.joannejacobs.com/2010/09/education-profs-dont-teach-tradecraft October 1, 2010.

Katz, M.B. (1973). *Class, bureaucracy & schools.* New York: Praeger Publishers.

Kendall, B. (2011, August 9). For-profit educator is sued. *The Wall Street Journal*, B2.

Kendall, B. & Sherr, I. (2010, August 31). H-P settles case for $55 million. *The Wall Street Journal,* B3.

Kincheloe, J. & Steinberg, S. (1997). Who said it can't happen here. In J.L. Kincheloe, S. R. Steinberg, & A.D. Gresson III (Eds.) *Measured lies: The bell curve examined.* (pp.3-50), New York: St. Martin's Press.

Klein, J. (2010, December 4-5). What I learned at the education barricades. *The Wall Street Journal*, A13.

Klein, J. (2011, May 10). Scenes from the New York education wars. *The Wall Street Journal,* A15.

Klein, J. (2012, September 17). A watershed for democrats and unions. *The Wall Street Journal,* A19.

Korn, M. (2010, August 17). For-profit schools fret over repayment test. *The Wall Street Journal,* B6.

Korn, M. (2012, October 25). For-profits' tough course. *The Wall Street Journal*, B1, B4.

Krehely, J., House, M., & Kernan, E. (2004). *Axis of ideology: Conservative foundations and public policy.* Washington, DC: National Committee for Responsive Philanthropy.

Krippendorff, K. (1980). *Content analysis: An introduction to its methodology.* Beverly Hills, CA: Sage.

Krugman, P.(2007, February 17). Who was Milton Friedman? *The New York Review of Books*, 54, (2), 27-30.

Kumar, R. (2012). Neoliberal education and imagining strategies of resistance: An introduction. In R. Kumar (Ed.) *Education and the reproduction of capital: Neoliberal knowledge and counterstrategies* (pp.1-14). New York: Palgrave Macmillan.

Kumashiro, K.K. (2008). *The seduction of common sense: How the right has framed the debate on America's schools.* New York: Teachers College Press.

Labaree, D.E. (1988). *The making of an American high school. The credentials market and the Central High School of Philadelphia, 1838-1939.* New Haven, CT: Yale University Press.

Law, S. (2013, June 6). What Enron and the IRS have in common. *The Wall Street Journal,* A17.

Lawton, C. & Clark, D. (2007, August 17). Dell to restate 4 years of results. *The Wall Street Journal*, A3.

Levine, A. (2005). *Educating America's leaders.* Washington, D.C. The Education Schools Project.

Linebaugh, K. (2013, February 21). GE sues Whirlpool on cartel. *The Wall Street Journal,* B7.

Linebaugh, K., Lessin, J.E. & Yadron, D. (2013, May 21). Apple avoided taxes on overseas billions. *The Wall Street Journal*, A1-2.

Loftus, P. (2013, June 13). Pfizer, Takeda to receive $2.15 billion on patent claims. *The Wall Street Journal*, B2.

Lortie, D. (1969). The balance of control and autonomy in elementary school teaching. In Etzioni (Ed.) *The semi-professions and their organization: Teachers, nurses, social workers* (pp.1-53), New York: The Free Press.

Lumby, J., & English, F.W. (2009, April-June). From simplicism to complexity in leadership identity and preparation: exploring the lineage and dark secrets. *International Journal of Leadership in Education,* 12 (2), 95-114.

Luskin, D. (2011, May 25). Professors to Koch brothers: Take your green back. *The Wall Street Journal*, A15.

Madrick, J. (2011). *Age of greed: The triumph of finance and the decline of America, 1970 to the present.* New York: Alfred A. Knopf.

Maranto, R., Ritter, G. and Levine, A. (2010, January 6). The future of ed. Schools: Five lessons from business schools. *Education Week*, 29 (16), 36.

Marglin, S.A. (2009, February 27). Why economists are part of the problem. *The Chronicle Review,* B7-B10.

Martin, S. (2012, August 10). Google agrees to record $22.5m fine. *USA Today.* 1B.

Martinez, B. & Saul, M.H. (2010, November 10). New York City Schools chancellor moves on. *The Wall Street Journal*, A4.

Maxwell, L. (2006, December 20). Finn basks in role as standards-bearer, gadfly. *Education Week*, 26 (16). 1, 26.

McGurn, W. (2002, March 20). Philadelphia dims Edison's light. *The Wall Street Journal*, A22.

McGurn, W. (2010, July 27). Giving lousy teachers the boot. *The Wall Street Journal*, A17.

McCarthy, T (1989). *The critical theory of Jurgen Habermas.* Cambridge, MA: MIT Press.

McWhirter, C. (2013, January 19-20). Ex-New Orleans major indicted for corruption. *The Wall Street Journal*, A.6.

Mead, J. & Green, P.C. (2012). Can charters and equity goals coexist? National Education Policy Center. Retrieved at http://nepc.colorado.edu/publication/chartering-equity on February 21, 2012.

Merton, R.K. (1968). *Social theory and social structure.* New York: The Free Press.

Messerli, J.(1972). *Horace Mann: A biography.* New York: Alfred A. Knopf.

Miller, V.W. (2012). The Broad challenge to democratic leadership: The other crisis in education. *Democracy & Education*, 20 (2), 1-11.

Mintzberg, H., (1983). *Structure in fives: Designing effective organizations.* Englewood Cliffs, NJ: Prentice-Hall, Inc.

Miron, G. (2010). New KIPP study underestimates attrition effects. National Education Policy Center. Retrieved at epic@colorado.edu on June 22.

Miron, G. & Nelson, C. (2002). *What's public about charter schools? Lessons learned about choice and accountability.* Thousand Oaks, CA: Corwin Press.

Mock, V. (2012, December 6). Cartel fixed prices for displays. *The Wall Street Journal*, B1.

Molnar, A. (2005). *School commercialism: From democratic ideal to market commodity.* New York: Routledge.

Monahan, T. (2005). *Globalization, technological change, and public education.* New York: Routledge.

Monga, V. (2013, May 21). Firing at golden parachutes. *The Wall Street Journal*, B4.

Moore, S. (2013, May 30). What would Milton Friedman say? *The Wall Street Journal,* A13.

Mullen, C.A., Samier, E.A., Brindley, S., English, F.W., & Carr, N.K. (2012 ). An espitemic frame analysis of neoliberal culture and politics in the US, UK, and the UAE. *Interchange*, 43 (3), 187-228.

Mullins, B. (2013, May 16). Former education official faces federal investigation. *The Wall Street Journal*, A6.

Murdoch, R. (2010, October 8). If schools were like' American idol'. *The Wall Street Journal*, A19.

Murray, C. (2005). The hallmark of the underclass. *The Wall Street Journal*, p. A18.

*New York Times* (2013, May 26). 'A' is for avoidance. P. 10.

National Education Policy Center (2010a, April 29). Think tank research: Policy makers should beware. Retrieved May 3, 2010 at www.thinktankreview.org

National Education Policy Center (2010b). Campaign to market Florida's grab-bag of reforms is an exercise in misused data: Heritage report is latest in a series of misleading analyses. Retrieved November 30, 2010 at http://nepc.colorado.edu/thinktank/learning-from-florida

National Education Policy Center (2010c). If I say it enough, will it still be untrue award. Retrieved on February 2, 2011 at http://nepc.colorado.edu/think-tank.bunkum-awards/2010.

National Education Policy Center (2011a). U.S. Department of Education big winner in 2010 Bunkum awards. Retrieved at http:// nepc.colorado.eu.reviews-obama-administrators-six-research-summaries on February 2, 2011.

National Education Policy Center (2011b). New Win-Win report on school vouchers still not a winner. Retrieved on April 19, 2011 at http://nepc.colorado.edu/thinktank/review-win-win-solution.

National Education Policy Center (2011c). Superintendent's survey doesn't support Fordham's conclusions. Retrieved on May 3, 2011 at http://nepc.colorado.edu.thinktank/review-ohio-superintendents.

National Education Policy Center (2011d), Exponentially flimsy: Report presents no evidence to support its call to grow the charter school sector like a mold or cancer. Retrieved at http://tinyurl.com/3millyoe on April 21, 2011.

National Education Policy Center (2011e). Gates report touting 'value-added' reached wrong conclusion. Retrieved on http://nepc.colorado.edu/thinktank/review-learning-about-teaching on January 13, 2011.

National Education Policy Center (2011f), California charter schools don't narrow black-white achievement gap. Retrieved on http://nepc.colorado.edu/thinktank/review-chartering-and-choice on November 10, 2011.

National Education Policy Center (2012, January 5). Despite tough times and tight school budgets, private education management organizations continue to grow-but results are mixed. Retrieved on January 5, 2012 at http://nepc.colorado.edu/publication/EMO-profiles-10-11.

Orden, E. & Gardiner, S. (2013, May 9). Corruption cases swell in New York legislature. *The Wall Street Journal,* A4.

Papa, R. (2011). Standards for educational leadership: Promises, paradoxes and pitfalls, pp. 195-209. In F. English (Ed.) *Handbook of Educational leadership, 2nd Edition.* Thousand Oaks, CA: Sage Publications, Inc.

Papa, R., English, F., Davidson, F., Culver, M. & Brown, R. (2013). *Contours of great leadership: The science, art, and wisdom of outstanding practice.* Lanham, MD: Rowman & Littlefield Publishers, Inc.

Parsons, T. (1951). *Structure and process in modern societies.* New York: The Free Press.

Parsons, T. (1967). *The social system.* Toronto, Canada. Collier-Macmillan.

Pasztor, A. (2013, March 4). Pratt & Whitney reveals faulty testing. *The Wall Street Journal*, B2.

Patterson, S. & Fitzpatrick, D. (2013, March 16-17). Senate puts 'whale' on the grill. *The Wall Street Journal,* B1-B2.

Pini, M. (2001, April). Moving public schools toward for-profit management. Privatizing the public sphere. Paper presented at the Annual Meeting of the American Educational Research Association, Seattle, WA.( ERIC Document Reproduction Service No. ED453603).

Plitt, M.B. (2011, March 30). Ex-D.C. schools leader must take tests blame. *USA Today retrieved athttp://www.usatoday.com/news/opinion/letters/2011-03-31_ST1_N.htm.*

Pollack, A. & Secret, M. (2012). Amgen agrees to pay $762 million for marketing anemia drug for off-label use. *The New York Times*, B3.

Powell, D. (2011, August 24). Finding hope in Atlanta. *Education Week*, 31 (1), 30.

Randall, M. J. & Johnson, A.R. (2012, October 2). AmEx set to pay over card claims. *The Wall Street Journal,* C1.Ravitch, D. (2000). *Left back: A century of battles over school reform.* New York: Simon & Schuster.

Ravitch, D. (2000). *Left back: A century of battles over school reform.* New York: Simon and Schuster.

Ravitch, D. (2005, May 12). Would you want to study at a Bloomberg school? *The Wall Street Journal*, A16.

Ravitch, D. (2010). *The death and life of the great American school system: How testing and choice are undermining education.* New York: Basic Books.

Rawls, J. (2003). *Justice as fairness: A restatement.* E. Kelly (Ed.). Cambridge, MA: Harvard University Press.

ReclaimAERA. (2013, May 1). *ReclaimAERA: In defense of research, education, and action for the public good.* Retrieved from http://reclaimaera.wordpress.com/

Rhee, M. (2011, January 11). In budget crises, an opening for school reform. *The Wall Street Journal*, A-17.

Rice, A. (2011, August 24). Poll finds Americans trust teachers, divided on unions. *Education Week,* 31 (1),16.

Richardson, J. (2011, September). Drip, drip, drip. *Phi Delta Kappan,* 93 (1), 4.

Ricker, M., Johnson, A.R. & Zibel, A. (2012, July 19). Capital one nailed on card sales ploys. *The Wall Street Journal,* C1-C2.

Riley, N.S. (2009, August 29-30). "We're in the venture philanthropy business" *The Wall Street Journal,* A11.

Riley, J.L. (2011, March 26-27). Weingarten for the union defense. *The Wall Street Journal,* A18.

Riley, N.S. (2012, October 27-28). Meet one of the Super-PAC men. *The Wall Street Journal,* A13.

Robelen, E.W. (2006, December 20). A think tank takes the plunge. *Education Week,* 26 (16), 26-29.

Rothstein, R. (2004). *Class and schools: Using social, economic, and educational reform to close the black-white achievement gap.* New York: Teachers College Press.

Saario, J. (2012, May 27). Cheating came in many shades. *The Atlanta Journal-Constitution,* B6.

Sahlberg, P. (2011). *Finnish lessons.* New York: Teachers College: Columbia University Press.

Saltman, K.J. (2005). *The Edison schools: Corporate schooling and the assault on public education.* Routledge, New York.

Saltman, K. J. (2012). The rise of venture philanthropy and the ongoing neoliberal assault on public education: The Eli and Edythe Broad Foundation (pp. 55-78). In W. Watkins (Ed.). *The assault on public education: Confronting the politics of corporate school reform.* New York: Teachers College Press.

Samuels, C.A. (2011, October 19). Broad prize. Do the successes spread? *Education Week,* 31(8), 1, 14.

Sanchez, C. (2013, April 10). El Paso schools cheating scandal: Who's accountable? National Public Radio and the *El Paso Times.* Retrieved at Google: El Paso School Cheating Scandal on June 13, 2013.

Sandel, M.J. (2012). *What money can't buy: The moral limits of markets.* New York: Farrar, Straus and Giroux.

Sawchuk, S. (2010, September 29). Study casts cold water on bonus pay. *Education Week,* 39 (5). 1, 12.

Sawchuk, S. (2012, May 16). New breed of advocacy groups shakes up education field. *Education Week,* 31 (31), 1, 16-18.

Schroeder, R. (1992). *Max Weber and the sociology of culture.* London: SAGE.

Schwartz, N.D. (2013, May 21). Apple avoids billions in taxes, Congressional panel says. *Pittsburgh Post Gazette,* A-4.

Scott, C.W. & Hill, C.M. (1954). *Public education under criticism.* New York: Prentice-Hall, Inc.

Smith, B. (2008, February). Deregulation and the new leader agenda: Outcomes and lessons from Michigan. *Educational Administration Quarterly,* 44 (1), 30-65.

Smith, R. (2010, April 9). Prince shows shame, Rubin defiance. *The Wall Street Journal,* C3.

Sparks, S.D. (2010, September 29). Think tank critics plant a stake in policy world. *Education Week,* 30 (5), 1, 14-15.

Spring, J. (1989). *The sorting machine revisited: National educational policy since 1945.* New York: Longman.

Stager, G. (2008, April). Public schools? *District administration,* 38.

Stern, S. (2013, April 12). Rewarding educators who cheat. *The Week,* 13 (612), 10.

Stiglitz, J.E. (2012). *The price of inequality: How today's divided society endangers out future.* New York: W.W. Norton & Company.

Stout, L.A. (2007, September 27). Corporations shouldn't be democracies. *The Wall Street Journal,* A17.

Strauss, V. (2013, March 4). Big outside money pouring into L.A. school board races. *The Washington Post.* Retrieved March 6, 2013, from http://www.washingtonpost.com/blogs/answer-sheet.

Sullo, B.(2011, April 17). The legacy of fear: test scores rise in Washington, D.C. (As does Suspicion). Retrieved at http://www.fundersanding.com/spotlight/the-legacy-fear-test-scores-rise-in-washington

Thomas B. Fordham Institute & Broad Foundation (2003). *Better leaders for America's schools: A manifesto.* Retrieved February 11, 2004, from www.edexcellencemedia.net/publications/2003/200305_betterleaders/manifesto.pdf.

Thurm, S. & Ng, S. (2013, May 6). Stock buybacks propel executive bonuses. *The Wall Street Journal,* B1-2.

Tyack, D. (1974). *The one best system: A history of American urban education.* Cambridge, MA: Harvard University Press.

Ujifusa, A. (2013, February 20). Jeb Bush-linked group gnawed on by watchdog. *Education Week,* 32 (21), 22-23.

Vincent, W. (1959). Book Review. Administrative behavior in education. *Teachers College Record,* 60 (4), 234-244.

*Wall Street Journal* (2011, October 21). Charters and minority progress. A14.

Watkins, W.H. (2012). The new social order: An educator looks at economics, politics, and race. In W.H. Watkins (Ed.) *The assault on public education: Confronting the politics of corporate school reform* (pp.7-37). New York: Teachers College Press.

Weber, M. (1930). *The Protestant ethic and the spirit of capitalism* (London: Allen and Unwin.

Weber, M. (1946). In H.H. Gerth & C. W. Mills (Eds and Trans.) *From Max Weber: Essays in sociology.* New York: Oxford University Press.

*Webster's seventh new collegiate dictionary.* Springfield, MA: G. & C. Merriam Company, Publishers.

Weeds, J. (2006, January 13). Opportunity, ease, encouragement, and shame: a short course in pitching for-profit. Education. *The Chronicle Review,* B10-B11.

Weinberg, N. (2003, October 6). Educating Eli. *Forbes,* 106-110.

Weingarten, R. (2011, April 25). Markets aren't the education solution. *The Wall Street Journal,* A15.

Whalen, J. (2011, November 4). Glaxo to pay U.S. $3 billion to settle. *The Wall Street Journal,* B3.

Whalen, J., Barrett, D. & Loftus, P. (2012, July 3). Glaxo sets guilty plea, $3 billion settlement. *The Wall Street Journal,* B1.

Wikipedia (2010). Eli Broad. Retrieved June 14, 2010 from http://en.wikipedia.org/wiki/Eli_Broad.

Wilkinson, R. & Pickett, K. (2009). *The spirit level: Why greater equality makes societies stronger.* New York: Bloomsbury Press.

Wilson, R. (2010, February 12). For-profit colleges change higher education's landscape. *The Chronicle of Higher Education,* 56 (22), A1, A16.

Wingfield, K. (2011, July 16-17). When teachers cheat—and then blame the tests. *The Wall Street Journal,* A11.

Winkler, R. (2010, August 21-22). For-profit schools put in detention. *The Wall Street Journal,* B16.

Wolcott, H.F. (1977). *Teachers versus technocrats: An educational innovation in anthropological perspective.* Eugene, Oregon: Center for Educational Policy and Management.

Wolff, M. (2008). *The man who owns the news: Inside the secret world of Rupert Murdoch.* New York: Broadway Books.

Woods, J. (2006, January 13). Opportunity, ease, encouragement, and shame: a short course in pitching for-profit education. *The Chronicle Review,* B10.

Woods, P.A. (2005). *Democratic leadership in education.* London: Paul Chapman.

Worthen, B. (2011, October 7). Oracle pays $199.5 million to settle U.S. fraud case. *The Wall Street Journal,* B3.

Zimmerman, A. (2013, February 15). Tiffany sues Costco on alleged fakes. *The Wall Street Journal,* B3.

Zimmerman, A. (2011, January 12). Mud flies in new Bratz brawl. *The Wall Street Journal,* B7.

# ABOUT THE AUTHORS

*Fenwick W. English,* the 16th recipient of the Living Legend Award from NCPEA, is the R. Wendell Eaves Senior Distinguished Professor of Educational Leadership in the School of Education at the University of North Carolina at Chapel Hill, a position he has held since 2001.

Dr. English is the epitome of the NCPEA practitioner/scholar, having begun his educational career as a third grade classroom teacher in 1961 in the Los Angeles City Schools, California. His career trajectory included stints as a secondary school teacher in Los Angeles County and experience as an assistant principal and principal there as well. He earned his B.S. and M.S. degrees in English literature and elementary school administration from the University of Southern California.

Following his Ph.D. in secondary education from the College of Education at Arizona State University in 1972, Dr. English became assistant superintendent in the Sarasota County Schools, Florida and within two years Superintendent of Schools in Hastings-on-Hudson, New York. Later, he went to Washington, D.C. and became Associate Executive Director of the American Association of School Administrators (the AASA) with a special emphasis on professional development for superintendents in the improvement of curriculum design and delivery. He also worked in the private sector as a manager then partner in the firm of Peat, Marwick, Mitchell & Co. (now KPMG Peat Marwick) in elementary and secondary education management practices consulting division of the Washington, D.C. office. He is acknowledged as the "father" of the national curriculum management audit which he pioneered in Columbus, Ohio in 1979.

Dr. English began his higher education teaching and research career in educational leadership with a professorship in the School of Education at Lehigh University in 1984. This placement was followed by a department chair position at the University of Cincinnati and later a professorship at the University of Kentucky where he was involved with doctoral programming via distance education. He became Dean of the School of Education at Indiana University-Purdue University, Fort Wayne, Indiana and later Vice-Chancellor of Academic Affairs there under the overall management direction of Purdue University. In 1988 Dr.

English was cited in *The Executive Educator* magazine published by the National School Boards Association as one of the nation's top six educational consultants.

Dr. English's record of research and publication includes authoring/co-authoring 35 books, over 100 articles in professional journals, as well as refereed research papers given at the American Education Research Association Divisions A and L; National Council of Professors of Educational Administration (NCPEA); University Council of Educational Administration (UCEA); British Educational Leadership and Management Association (BELMAS) and CCEAM (Commonwealth Council of Educational Administration and Management). He has conducted on-site research which has been subsequently published in academic journals in educational leadership in he United States, England and Australia. He has been recognized by his colleagues as a national leader by serving as President of UCEA 2006-07 and of NCPEA 2011-2012.

In the School of Education at UNC-Chapel Hill Dr. English teaches classes at the master's and doctoral levels in curriculum leadership, school system functions, advanced leadership theory and organizational theory. He has been twice nominated by his doctoral students for university recognition of excellence in doctoral mentoring in 2008 and 2013.

Some of the authored/co/authored recent scholarly books by Dr. English are: *Contours of Great Leadership* (2013) with R. Papa (Sr. Author.), and F. Davidson, M. Culver and R. Brown. Lanham, MD: Rowman and Littlefield Publishers; *Educational Leadership at 2050: Conjectures, Challenges, and Promises* (2012) with, R. Papa, C.A. Mullen, & T. Creighton,. Lanham, MD: Rowman & Littlefield Publishers; *The Art of Educational Leadership: Balancing Performance and Accountability* (2008) SAGE Publishing Company of Thousand Oaks, California; and *Anatomy of Professional Practice: Promising Research Perspectives on Educational Leadership* (2008) released by Rowman and Littlefield Publishers. He has been a long time critic of the standardization of educational leadership and preparation (English, 2000; 2003; 2008; 2012).

Research and scholarship published internationally by Dr. English include (2012) "Bourdieu's misrecognition: Why educational leadership standards will not reform schools or leadership," *Journal of Educational Administration and History,* 44 (2), 155-170; with L.C. Ehrich (Australian Sr. Author) (2012), "What can grassroots leadership teach us about school leadership? " *Halduskultuur-Administrative Culture* 13 (2), 85-108; with C. Bolton (Sr. Author from the UK) (2010), "De-Constructing the Logic/Emotion Binary in Educational Preparation and Practice," *Journal of Educational Administration* 48, 5, 561-578; and with J. Lumby (Sr.Author from the UK) (2009), "From Simplicism to Complexity in Leadership Identity And Preparation: Exploring the Lineage and Dark Secrets," *International Journal of Leadership in Education,* 12 (2), 95-114.

***Rosemary Papa***, Foreword

Dr. Papa is a former NCPEA Living Legend (2003) and presently the Del and Jewell Lewis Endowed Chair in Learning Centered Leadership Professor, Educational Leadership at Northern Arizona University.

***Carol A. Mullen***, Epilogue

Dr. Mullen served as the NCPEA president (2012-2013) and is Professor of Educational Leadership, Director of the School of Education, and Associate Dean for Professional Education of the College of Liberal Arts and Human Sciences at Virginia Tech.

# APPENDIX A
## A Record of the Career Trajectories of the Broad Superintendent's Academy Graduates 2004-2011

By Zan Crowder, Ph.D. Graduate Assistant
University of North Carolina at Chapel Hill

| Name | Grad Yr. | Prior Background | Placement Coincident with Broad training | 4/2012 Position | 3/2013 Position |
|---|---|---|---|---|---|
| Alfaro, Robert | 2004 | Assoc. Superintendent, San Antonio ISD | Regional Superintendent, Clark County (NV) Schools (2005) | Director Urban Accounts, Renaissance Learning | No Change |
| Anderson, Bart G. | 2006 | Superintendent, Port Clinton City Schools (OH) (2001-2004) | | Superintendent, Education Services Center of Central Ohio (2004-Present) | Doctoral degree controversy- Resigned from Ed. Services, 2/13 |
| Atkinson, Cheryl L.H. | 2006 | | Superintendent, Lorain City Schools (OH) | Superintendent, DeKalb County Schools (GA)(9/2011-Present) | Resigned from DeKalb, 2/13 |
| Avossa, Robert | 2011 | Teacher track. Chief Strategy and Accountability Officer, Charlotte-Mecklenburg Schools (NC) | Superintendent, Fulton County Schools (GA) (6/2011) | Superintendent, Fulton County Schools (GA)(2011-present) | No Change |

| Name | Year | Prior Position | | Position | Status |
|---|---|---|---|---|---|
| Baker, Jill A. | 2005 | Principal, Long Beach USD (CA) | | Assist. Superintendent, Long Beach USD (CA) | Chief Academic Officer LBUSD |
| Barbic, Chris | 2011 | Founder and CEO, YES Prep Public Schools (TX) (1998) | | Superintendent, Achievement School District (TN) (5/2011-present) | No Change |
| Barry, John | 2004 | Maj. General, Air Force (retired 2004) | | Superintendent, Aurora Public Schools (CO) (2006-present) | Announced retirement from Aurora, 7/13 |
| Bass, Angela | 2005 | Superintendent of Instruction, LAUSD (CA) | | Executive Director, San Diego USD (CA) (2010-present) | No Change |
| Blakeney Clark, Anne | 2010 | Teacher Track Regional Superintendent, Charlotte-Mecklenburg Schools (NC) | | Chief Academic Officer, Charlotte-Mecklenburg Schools (NC) | No Change---Entire career at CMS |
| Blaine, Jennifer | 2010 | Teacher track, Aldine ISD (TX) | | Assoc. Superintendent, Spring Branch ISD (TX) (2002-present) | No Change |
| Boasberg, Tom | 2009 | VP for Corporate Development, Level 3 Communications; legal advisor, FCC | | Superintendent, Denver Public Schools (CO) (2009-present) | No Change |
| Bobb, Robert C. | 2005 | City Manager, Oakland, Richmond, Santa Ana, Kalamazoo; CEO The Robert Bobb Group, LLC. | President, Washington DC Board of Education | Emergency Financial Manager, Detroit Public Schools | CEO LAPA Group, LLC, consulting |
| Boone, Melinda | 2004 | Speech Pathologist, Suffolk Public Schools | CAO Norfolk Public Schools | Superintendent, Worcester Public Schools (MA) (2009-present) | No Change |
| Brady, Thomas | 2004 | Colonel, US Army; COO, Fairfax Co PS; COO SD of Philadelphia; COO, Washington | Superintendent, Providence SD (2008-2011) | COO, Gems Ed. 2011-2012 | Resigned Superint |

| | | | DC Schools | | | endency of Providence Schools with time remaining on contract. Now Tom Brady and Associates, consulting, 2012 |
|---|---|---|---|---|---|---|
| Brandon, Yvonne W. | 2006 | | Dep. Superintendent, Richmond Schools (VA) | Superintendent, Richmond Schools (VA) (2009-present) | No Change. |
| Brizard, Jean-Claude | 2007 | Regional Superintendent, NYC DOE | Superintendent, Rochester Schools (NY) | Superintendent, Chicago Public Schools (IL) (4/2011-present) | Lasted 17 months as Chicago CEO. Resigned, 10/2012 |
| Brown, Mark | 2011 | Brig. General, US Air Force | | | |
| Burt, Helen | 2004 | Board Officer TXU Energy | | Senior VP, Pacific Gas and Electric Company (CA) | No Change |
| Burt, Walter | 2002 | | Superintendent, Pontiac SD (MI) (1999-2003) | Professor, Western Michigan | Interim Dean, Western Michigan, 2012 |
| Byas, Dennis D. | 2005 | Superintendent, Colton Joint USD (CA) | | Superintendent, San Lorenzo USD (CA) (2009-present) | No Change |
| Bynum, Randolph | 2007 | Battle Executive Officer, US Army | CAO, Charleston Co SD; Associate Superintendent, Atlanta PS (2008-2011) | Superintendent, Sumter Co. Schools (SC) (7/2011-present) | No Change |
| Carney, Ingrid | 2007 | Senior Executive Director Chicago Leadership Academies | Deputy Superintendent, | President, National Staff Development | Consulting, No |

| | | (2001-2005) | Boston Public Schools (MA) (2005-2008) | Council & CEO, Carney for Kids Education Consulting Group | Change |
|---|---|---|---|---|---|
| Carter, Arnold Woodrow | 2002 | Colonel, US Army; Superintendent, Bourbon Co. Schools (KY) | | | Superintendency terminated by Capistrano USD in 2009. |
| Cerf, Christopher | 2004 | CEO Sangari Global Education; COO Edison Schools | Deputy Chancellor NYC DOE (2004-2009) | Acting Commissioner of Education, NJ (2011-present) | No Change |
| Coleman-Potter, Bonita | 2008 | Deputy Superintendent, Jackson Public Schools (MS) | | Deputy Superintendent, Prince George's Co. Public Schools | Superintendent, Ocean Springs SD, 6/2012-Present |
| Contreras, Sharon | 2010 | CEO, Providence Schools (RI) (2008-2011) | Superintendent, Syracuse SD (7/2011-present) | Superintendent, Syracuse SD (7/2011-present) | No Change |
| Covington, John | 2008 | Superintendent, Kansas City Public Schools (MO) | | Chancellor, Michigan Education Achievement Authority (2011-present) | No Change |
| Darden, Thomas | 2009 | Managing Director, Reliant Equity Investors | Deputy for Process Improvement and Compliance, SD of Philadelphia | Deputy Chief, Strategic Programs, SD of Philadelphia | Resigned from Philadelphia, 7/12 |
| Dawning, Paula | 2002 | Sales Executive, AT&T | | Superintendent, Benton Harbor Area Schools (MI) (2007) | Independent Ed. Management Professional 2012 |
| Deasy, John E. | 2006 | Superintendent, Prince George's County Public Schools (MD) | Deputy Director of Education Division, Gates Foundation | Superintendent, Los Angeles USD | No Change |
| Dilworth, John | 2005 | Superintendent, Montgomery Public Schools (AL) | | Superintendent, E. Baton Rouge (2009-2012) | Resigned Superintendency, |

| | | | | | E Baton Rouge, Feb. 24, 2012 |
|---|---|---|---|---|---|
| Downing, Kathryn M. | | CEO, LA Times | | Social Venture Partners Santa Barbara | SVP--investments |
| Evans, Mark A. | 2003 | Managing Principal, Bancroft Research Group | | Superintendent, Andover Public Schools (KA) (2005-2013) | Superintendent, Omaha Schools, 2013 |
| Fryer, Lawrence W. Jr. | 2006 | Officer, US Marine Corps; Senior Program Manager, CACI, Int. Inc.; Senior Managing Consultant, IBM | COO, Prince George's Co. Public Schools (2007-2011) | Chief Operating Officer, Austin ISD (TX) 2010-present) | No Change |
| Gilbert, Silvanus Taco | 2010 | Commandant, Air Force Academy | | Director of Strategic Planning, Sierra Nevada Corporation | Private Industry |
| Gill, Paul | 2007 | Air Force Officer and Senior VP for American Dental Partners | COO, Pittsburgh Public Schools (PA) (2008) | Assistant Superintendent, Alvord USD (CA) (2009-present) | No Change |
| Gist, Deborah | 2008 | State Superintendent of Education, Washington DC (2007) | | Commissioner, Rhode Island Department of Elementary and Secondary Education (2009-present) | No Change |
| Glascoe, Michael E. | 2002 | Assistant Superintendent for Educational Accountability, Fairfax Co. Public Schools (VA) (1999-2005) | | Interim Director, National School Boards Association (2011) | Resigned admist controversy from Supt. Of Paterson, NJ schools in 2008; now The Legacy Group, consulting 2012 |
| Goodloe-Johnson, Maria | 2003 | | Superintendent, Charleston School District (2003-2005); | Deputy Chancellor, Detroit Public Schools | Dismissed in wake of financial |

| | | | Superintendent, Seattle (2007-2011) | | scandal from Seattle Superintendency in 2011; Now Deceased |
|---|---|---|---|---|---|
| Gorman, Peter | 2004 | Chief Operating Officer, Orange County Public Schools (FL) | Superintendent, Charlotte-Mecklenburg Public Schools (2006-2011) | Vice President, Education Division, News Corporation | Also, Consultant, DMC (District Managing Council) |
| Green, Patricia | 2002 | Administrator, Prince George's Co. PS & North Allegheny SD | | Superintendent, Ann Arbor Public Schools (2011-present) | No Change |
| Hammond, James Quezon | 2010 | Superintendent, Davis Joint USD (CA) (2007-2010) | | Superintendent, Ontario-Montclair School District (CA) (2010-present) | No Change |
| Hankins, Paul | 2004 | Brig. General, US Air Force | | President, Association of Alabama Independent Colleges and Universities | No Change — Professional Organization |
| Hanna, Thomas | 2008 | | The School District of Philadelphia (2008-2011) | Chief of Innovation, NYC DOE (2011-present) | No Change |
| Harner,, William E. | 2005 | Lt. Colonel, US Army Superintendent, New Orleans Recovery SD | Deputy CEO, The School District of Philadelphia (2006) | Superintendent, Cumberland Valley School District (PA) (2008-present) | Resigned from Supt. In Greenville, SC prior to contract expiration. |
| Harries, Garth | 2009 | McKinsey Consultant & Asst. Superintendent NYC COE (2003-2009) | | Assistant Superintendent of Portfolio and Performance, New Haven School District (CT) | Possible Movement in 2013 with retireme |

85

| | | | | | |
|---|---|---|---|---|---|
| | | | | (2009-present) | nt of New Haven Superintendent |
| Harris, Carl | 2002 | Superintendent, Franklin Co. Schools (NC) (199402004) | | Deputy Assistant Secretary for Policy, US DOE (2010-persent) | Consultant, TE21 |
| Hayes, Aaron B. | 2005 | | | | |
| Heatley, Edmond T. | 2008 | Teacher track and former Marine. Superintendent, Chino Valley USD (CA) | | Superintendent, Clayton County School District (GA) (2009-2012) | Left Clayton, 2012 February, 2013, withdrew from Berkeley USD job hunt. |
| Hegedus, Andrew S. | 2005 | | | Executive Director, Organizational Development, Christina School District (DE) (2004 to present) | Sr. Research Manager, Kingsbury Center, Educational think tank |
| Heiligenstein, Anne | 2010 | Commissioner of Texas Department of Family and Protective Services; Director of health and Human Services Policy for Gov. George Bush | | Retired | |
| Heyer, Erik | 2003 | Investment Executive, Goldman Sachs, New Mountain Capital | | Founder, Auburn School (VA) (2009), Siena School (MD) (2006), Victory Schools | Entrepreneur—No Change |
| Hite, William R. Jr. | 2005 | | Deputy Superintendent, Prince George's County Public Schools (MD) | Superintendent, Prince George's County Public Schools (MD) (2009-present) | Superintendent, Philadelphia 7/2012 |
| Hopkins, Delores | 2002 | Assistant Superintendent, Jackson Public Schools (MS) | | | |
| Hughey, Gary | 2005 | Chief Operating Officer, St. Louis School District (2005) | | | Legal actions |

| | | | | | concerning termination from St. Louis |
|---|---|---|---|---|---|
| Hurt, Dorene | 2009 | Colonel, US Army | Faculty, Industrial College of the Armed Forces | | |
| Ingram, Alan | 2007 | Chief Master Sergeant, US Air Force | Chief Academic Officer, Oklahoma City Public Schools | Superintendent, Springfield School District (MA) (2008-2012; will depart at end of contract, 6/2012) | Deputy Commissioner, DOE/maryland 6/12 |
| Jenkins, Barbara | 2006 | Teacher track. Assistant Superintendent for Human Resources, Charlotte-Mecklenburg Public Schools | | Superintendent, Orange County Public Schools (FL) (3/2012) | No Change |
| Jenney, Timothy | 2002 | Superintendent, Virginia Beach School District (1996-2005) | | Superintendent, Fort Bend ISD (TX) (2006-present) | Conflict of interest scandal. Retired 1/2013 |
| Johns, Christine | 2004 | Deputy Superintendent, Baltimore Co. Public Schools | | Superintendent, Utica Community Schools (MI) | No Change |
| Johnson, Melody | 2002 | | Superintendent, Providence Public Schools (RI) (2002-2005) | Scholar in Residence, Texas Christian University (2011-presen) | Abrupt resignation as Supt of Fort Worth Schools following budget discrepancies. Still at TCU. |
| King, Cheryl | 2003 | CAO, Providence Public Schools (RI) (2001-2004) | Director, Leadership for Learning Innovation, EDC (2004-present) | Distinguished Education Scholar, Education Development Center, Inc. (2004-present) | Research Foundation—No Change |
| Knighton, Christine (Nickey) | 2007 | Colonel, US Army | Chief HR Officer, Prince George's Co. Public Schools (2008-2009) | | Consultant, WINNERS |

| Name | Year | Position 1 | Position 2 | Position 3 | Position 4 |
|---|---|---|---|---|---|
| Lane, Linda | 2003 | Assistant Superintendent, Des Moines Schools (2007-2010) | | Superintendent, Pittsburgh Public Schools (2010-present) | No Change |
| Lee, Candy | 2004 | President, United Airlines Loyalty Services | | Chief Advisor and Developer, The Washington Post Masterclass | Professor, Medill Northwestern University |
| Leonard, Steven | 2002 | | | Assistant Superintendent, Tauton Public Schools (MA) | No Change |
| Lepper, Steven | 2009 | Maj. General, US Air Force | | | |
| Levenson, Nathan | 2004 | Assistant Superintendent, Harvard Public Schools | Superintendent, Arlington Public Schools (2005-2008) | Cofounder and Managing Director, District and Community Partners (2008-present) | Managing Director, DMC (District Managing Council) |
| Loe, Cynthia | 2004 | Teacher track. Assoc. Superintendent, Executive, Gwinnett Co. School District | Superintendent, Fulton Co PS (GA) (2008-2011) | Retired 2011 | |
| Lowery, Lillian | 2004 | Superintendent, Christina School District (DE) | | Secretary of Education, Delaware DOE (2009-present) | State Superintendent, Maryland DOE |
| Lusi, Susan | 2003 | VP of public policy at Alliance for Excellent Education | Superintendent, Portsmouth SD (RI) (2005-2011) | Superintendent, Providence Public Schools (RI) 2011-present) | No Change |
| Lyles, Marcia V. | 2006 | Regional Superintendent, Brooklyn | Deputy Chancellor for Teaching and Learning, NYC DOE | Superintendent, Christina School District (DE) (2009-2012) after contract expired | Superintendent, Jersey City Schools, 6/12 |
| MacCormick, Penny | 2011 | Chief Academic Officer, Hartford Public Schools (CT) | | Chief Academic Officer, New Jersey DOE (2011-2012) | Superintendent, Montclair SD, NJ |
| Malone, Matthew H. | 2003 | Superintendent, Swampscott Public Schools | Asst. Superintendent, San Diego ISD (CA) | Superintendent, Brockton School District (MA) (2009-2012) | |

| Name | Year | Position 1 | Position 2 | Position 3 | Position 4 |
|---|---|---|---|---|---|
| Manley, Paul | 2008 | Colonel, US Air Force | | Director of Business Development, L-3 | Director of Business Development, Viecore |
| Manos(-Sittnick), Angela M. | 2006 | Colonel, US Army | | Instructor, Universities of Phoenix, St Leo and Troy | |
| Martinez, Pedro | 2009 | Deputy Superintendent, Washoe Co. School District | | Deputy Superintendent, Clark County School District (2011-present) | Superintendent, Washoe SD 6/2012 |
| Materassi, Laura | 2003 | Special Asst to Barbara Byrd-Bennett, CEO Cleveland SD (OH) | | Highly paid consultancy work for Detroit Public Schools | |
| Matthews, Vincent C. | 2006 | NewSchools Venture Fund, Edison Schools | Regional Superintendent, Oakland USD (2007) | Superintendent, San Jose USD (2010-present) | No Change |
| Mazyck, Veleter | 2007 | General Counsel, Washington DC Public Schools (1999-2005) | General Counsel, Atlanta Public Schools(2005-2011) | Chief of Staff, US Representative Marcia Fudge | No Change |
| McCown, Gaynor | 2004 | | | Deceased | |
| McCann, Barbara | 2003 | Rear Admiral | Executive Director, Advanced Math and Science Academy Charter School | Retired | |
| McGinley, Nancy J. | 2002 | CEO Philadelphia Education Fund | | Superintendent, Charleston Co Public Schools (SC) (2007 to present) | No Change |
| McIntyre, James P. Jr. | 2006 | COO, Boston Public Schools | | Superintendent, Knox Co Public Schools (TN) (2008-present) | No Change |
| Melendez de Santa Ana, Thelma | 2006 | Superintendent, Pomona USD | Assistant Secretary, US DOE (2009-2011) | Superintendent, Santa Ana USD (2011-present) | No Change |
| Micheaux, Donna J. | 2005 | | CAO, Dallas ISD (TX) (2007-2011) | CEO, Micheaux, Inc. Consulting (2011-2012) | Asst. Executive Director |

|  |  |  |  |  | for Organizational Leadership and Development, Allegheny Intermediate Unit (2012-present) |
|---|---|---|---|---|---|
| Miles, Mike | 2011 | Army Ranger, Superintendent, Harrison School District (CO) | Superintendent, Dallas ISD (TX) (2012) | Superintendent, Dallas ISD (4/2012) | No Change |
| Mir, Gasper | 2003 | Owner, Accounting Firm MFR, PC | Executive Adviser, Houston ISD (2003-2008) | Chairman, Luby's Inc. |  |
| Moore, Reginald | 2005 | VP, BMC Software (1992-2003) |  | COO, Community Health, Houston |  |
| Morris, Howard | 2003 | Superintendent, Riverview SD (AR) |  | Superintendent, Riverview SD (AR) | Retired 12/12. 30 years service to Riverview |
| Morrison, Heath | 2009 | Superintendent, Washoe Co SD |  | Superintendent, Charlotte-Mecklenburg Schools (2012) | No Change |
| Munoz, Pablo | 2006 | Teacher track. |  | Superintendent, Elizabeth Public Schools (NJ) (2005-present) | No Change |
| Oats, Mike | 2011 | Lt. General, US Army |  | VP, Lockheed Martin |  |
| Oliver, Bernard | 2002 |  |  | Professor, College of Education, University of Florida | No Change |
| Olson, Kimberly | 2005 | Colonel, US Air Force; HR Director, Dallas ISD (TX) |  | Trustee, Weatherford ISD (TX) | Esecutive Director, Grace After Fire, Non-profit |

| | | | | | (2010-present) |
|---|---|---|---|---|---|
| Paquin, Natalye | 2004 | Counsel, Chicago Public Schools; Chief of Staff, SD of Philadelphia | COO, SD of Philadelphia(PA) (2004-2012) | CEO, Girl Scouts of Eastern Pennsylvania | No Change |
| Peebles, Thandiwe | 2002 | Teacher track. | CAO, Cleveland Public Schools (OH); Superintendent, Minneapolis Schools (2004-2006) | Consultant for Rockford Schools | Stormy tenure in Minnesota |
| Peppler, Judy | 2011 | State President, Qwest Communications | | Chief Transformation Officer, Wake Co public Schools (2011 to present) | Resigned Wake County 10/2012 |
| Pierce, Glenn R. | 2003 | Executive, Pizza Hut | VP and Chief Development Officer, Charter Schools USA | President and CEO, Pacific Charter School Development | CEO, Canyon-Agassi Charter School Facilities Fund (2010-present) |
| Pitre(-Martin), Maria | 2008 | Assistant Superintendent, E. Baton Rouge Parish (LA) | CAO, SD of Philadelphia | Director, K-12 Curriculum and Instruction, North Carolina Department of Public Instruction | No Change |
| Polakow-Suransky, Shael | 2008 | Deputy Chancellor, NYC DOE | | Chief Accountability Officer, NYC DOE (2011 to present) | Chief Academic Officer NYCDOE |
| Polk, Steven R. | 2006 | Lt. General, US Air Force | | Chairman of the Board, Sourcefire, Inc. Software and Security | |
| Pombar, Frank D. | 2008 | Air Force | Deputy Chief for Attendance and Truancy, SD of Philadelphia (2009) | | |
| Porter, John Q. | 2006 | | Superintendent, Oklahoma City Schools (OK) (2006-2008) | President, Mosaica Turnaround Partners | Resigned from Supt. In OK |

| | | | | | |
|---|---|---|---|---|---|
| | | | | | regarding misappropriation of funds; criminal investigation. Now Consulting, Mosaica |
| Purcell, Carlinda | 2004 | | Superintendent, Montgomery Co. SD (??-2006) | Interim Director, ENI | Mont. Co. tenure ended with early resignation at request of BOE; Now Superintendent, Reading SD (2012-present) |
| Randall (Hughes), Pamela R. | 2004 | Executive Administrator, St. Louis SD (2003-2005) | Instruction Officer, Chicago Public Schools (2006-2009) | School Improvement Officer, Houston ISD (2009-present) | No Change |
| Rayer, Ben | 2002 | Financial Consultant, Pulic Financial Management Teacher---Teach for America (1991-1993) | Chief Charter and New Schools Officer, SD of Philadelphia | Director, Rayer & Associates, education consulting | CEO Touchstone Education, Inc (2011-Present) |
| Raymond, Jonathan P. | 2006 | CAO, Charlotte-Mecklenbeurg Schools | | Superintendent, Sacramento City Schools (2009-present) | No Change |
| Redden, Joseph J. | 2003 | | Superintendent, Cobb Co SD (GA) | CEO Quality Education Data (5/2012) | Reisnged 2005 from Cobb under criminal investigation; |

| | | | | | now President ITEP--- Educational Technology |
|---|---|---|---|---|---|
| Richardson, Rick | 2011 | Colonel, US Army | | Superintendent, New Kent Co Schools (VA) (2007-present) | No Change |
| Robinson, Wendy | 2002 | | | Superintendent, Fort Wayne Community Schools (2003-present) | No Change |
| Roosevelt, Mark | 2003 | | Superintendent, Pittsburgh Schools (2005-2010) | President, Antioch College (OH) | |
| Rose, Joel | 2006 | Senior Executive, Edison Schools (1998-2006) | Executive positions, NYC DOE (2006-2011) | CEO, New Classrooms, blended learning program | Educational Entrepreneur |
| Rosen, Amy | 2004 | COO, New Visions for Public Schools | Founder, Public Private partnership Gourp | CEO, NFTE and Network for Teaching Entrepreneurship | Non-Profit |
| Rounds, Michael | 2010 | Genera, US Army | COO Kansas City SD (2010) | | Deputy Superintendent, Louisiana DOE (2012-present) |
| Rudden, Eileen | 2009 | VP, Avaya, Inc. internet technology | Chief of the Office of Specialized Services, Chicago Public Schools | Chief of Colleg and Career Preparation, Chicago Public Schools (2010-2012) | Board of Directors, KnowldegeWorks, 5/2012 |
| Runcie, Robert | 2009 | Chief Information Officer, Chicago Public Schools (2003) | | Superintendent, Broward Co Public Schools (FL) (2011-present) | No Change |
| Ryder, Beverly | 2006 | Executive, Edison International | Executive Director Parent Engagement, LAUSD | ??? | |
| Saavedra, | 2002 | Executive offices, Houston ISD | Superintendent, | Senior Advisor, | Consulti |

| | | | | | |
|---|---|---|---|---|---|
| Albelardo | | | Houston ISD (2004-2009) | The District Management Council | ng, No Change |
| San Pedro, Ofelia | 2005 | COO Kaplan Virtual Education | | Chief Financial Officer, Republica, LLC, marketing firm | Non-educational, No Change |
| Sandoval, Monica | 2003 | Executive offices, Houston ISD (1990's) | | Consultant, Kligo Consulting, Inc. (2006-present) | Consulting—No Change |
| Scanlan, John | 2007 | Captain, Navy | Deputy Superintendent, Rochester City SD | Chief Financial and Administrative Office, Cleveland Schools (2012) | Fired from Rochester with change in Supt. No Change |
| Scott, Irvin | 2010 | Executive Assistant Superintendent, Prince George's Co Public Schools (2007-2008) | Executive offices, Boston PS (2008-2011) | Deputy Director, Education, Gates Foundation (2011-present) | Non-profit, No Change |
| Shazor, Marilyn | 2010 | CEO, Metro Transit System, SW OH RTA (2006-2010 | | | Filed anti-discrimination lawsuit upon dismissal from Ohio RTA. |
| Sheffield, LaVonne | 2002 | Cleveland government under Mayor Michael White | Executive positions, E. Baton Rouge, Philadelphia, Detroit | Superintendent, Rockford SD (2009-2011) | Resigned during great discord. Now Associate VP, Jobs for the Future, Non-Profit |
| Silva, Valeria | 2008 | MN DOE | | Superintendent, St. Paul Public Schools (2009-present) | No Change |
| Sims, Deborah A. | 2005 | Deputy Superintendent, San Francisco USD | Superintendent, Antioch USD (2006-2010) | Asst. Superintendent, Fremont USD (CA) (2010- | Resignation after great controve |

| | | | | present) | rsy in Antioch. No Change |
|---|---|---|---|---|---|
| Spampinato, Lynn | 2004 | Superintendent, Summit SD (CO) (2003-2004) | Deputy Superintendent, Pittsburgh (2005-2006) | Consulting for Pittsburgh Schools (2008) | History of very short tenures and large buyouts; denied Virgin Islands appointment Consulting |
| Statham, Kimberly | 2003 | | Executive Offices, Oakland USD, Washington DC, Montgomery Co. SD | NewSchools Venture Fund/DC Schools Fund | Board of Trustees, FOCUS, Washington DC |
| Stecz, Terrence | 2007 | CEO/President, Edison Schools (2004-2006) | | CEO, LeadAmerica, Inc., educational venture capital (2010-Present) | Educational Leadership Programs for Students |
| Stockwell, Robert | 2002 | | Associate Superintendent, E. Baton Rouge Parish (retired 2008) | | |
| Tata, Anthony | 2009 | Brig. General, US Army | COO, Washington DC PS | Superintendent, Wake County PS (NC) (2011-2012) | Lasted 21 months. Fired as Wake Supt. 9/2012. Now Secretary of Transportation, North Carolina (2013) |
| Terry, Laverne | 2004 | | Assistant | Commissioner of | No |

| | | | Superintendent, Hartford SD | Education, Virgin Islands (2008-present) | Change |
|---|---|---|---|---|---|
| Torres, Jose M. | 2005 | Superintendent, San Ysidro SD (CA) | Regional Superintendent, Chicago PS | Superintendent, District U-46 (IL) (2008-present) | No Change |
| Van Valkenburg, Frederick D. | 2005 | Brig. General, US Air Force | | Deceased | |
| Vigil, Joseph | 2002 | | | Deceased | |
| Ward, Randolph | 2003 | | Executive, Oakland USD (2003-2006) | Superintendent, San Diego (2006 to present) | No Change |
| Wardynski, Casey | 2010 | Colonel, US Army | Chief Financial Officer, Aurora PS (2010-2011) | Superintendent, Huntsville Public Schools (2011-present) | No Change |
| Watkins, Patricia | 2002 | Superintendent, Prince Edwards Co. PS | | Superintendent, Hempstead Union Free SD (NY) (2009-present) | No Change |
| Wechsler, Norman | 2003 | Superintendent, Bronx High Schools (1999-2993) | | Coach/Facilitator, NYC Leadership Academy (2005-present) | No Change |
| Welch, John | 2002 | Financial analyst, Boeing; VP Business Services, Seattle Community College | Superintendent, Highline PS (WA) (2005-2011) | Superintendent, Puget Sound Educational Service District # 121(2011-Present) | No Change |
| Whalen, Kathleen | 2002 | | Chief of Staff, Sacramento USD (until 2003??) | | |
| White, John | 2010 | Exec Director, Teach for America (2003-2006); Deputy Chancellor for talkent, labor and innovation, NYC DOE (2006-???) | Superintendent, Recovery School District (LA) 5/2011-1/2012) | State Superintendent of Education (LA) (1/2012) | No Change |
| Wilkins, Stephen M. | 2007 | Colonel, US Army; Program Manager of Facilities, Chicago PS | Executive Director of Human Resources, Alexandria City PS (2009-2011) | COO, Division of Operations, DeKalb Co Schools (2012) | No Change |
| Williams, Bennie | 2007 | Maj. General, US Army | | Deceased | |
| Wise, John | 2003 | Extensive background: Superintendent, Duval Co PS, Christina SD; Executive positions, Anne Arundel, Charlotte-Mecklenburg Schools | | Managing Director, Atlantic Research Partners, LLC, leadership consulting | Education Entrepreneur |

**About this Appendix**

This appendix represents a preliminary investigation into the professional histories of Broad Superintendent graduates. The data presented were acquired primarily through online searches of professional social networks, school district websites, state DOE websites, press releases, traditional press sources, blogs and the Broad Foundation website. Such an investigation is warranted because the Broad Foundation provides detailed biographical information for only a select number of its graduates and, as a private foundation is not required by any oversight agency to reveal such information to the public howsoever intimately related and influential its graduates become within the sphere of public education. The authors acknowledge that the data reported in the Appendix are incomplete and contained in the paper, "Counterspin: A discourse analysis of Eli Broad's leadership brag sheet" given as a symposium paper at the American Education Research Association's Annual Conference in San Francisco, California in May of 2013, Session #70.013."

# INDEX

**A**
accreditation, 38
achievement gap, 46-47
Achilles, C., iv
Adams, R., 10
ahimsa, 53
Amazon, 13
American Education Research Association, 61
American Enterprise Institute, 7, 17
American Express Inc., 32
Amgen, 33
Anderson, G., 15
Andrews, A., 54
Apollo group, 37-38
Apple, Inc., 12, 23, 31, 34
Argosy University, 39
Argyris, C., 53
Aronson, L., 51
Art Institutes, 39
Atlanta, Georgia, cheating scandal, 45-46

**B**
background justice, concept of, 36, 59
Baer, J., 16
Banchero, S., 8, 17, 45, 49, 55-56
Baker, B., 51
Banjo, S., 33
Bank of America, 34
Bankston, C., 3
Barclays Bank, 30
Barrett, D., 32
Barry, B., 4, 22, 46-47
Beach, B., iv
Belkin, D., 40
*Bell Curve,* (the book), 17-18
Bello, M., 44
Bennett, W., 18
Berrett, D., 40
Bersin, A., 54
Big Sister Foundations, 8
billionaire boys club, 25, 52
Blau, P., 14
Blinder, A., 24, 43, 52
Bloomberg, M., 11
*Blueprint for Reform*, 51
Blumenstyk, G., 38, 40
Bolton, C., 79
bonus pay, for test scores, 44-45, 54, 58

Borg, W., 25
Borja, R., 18, 38
Boudon, R., 54
Bourdieu, P., 1, 4, 6, 14, 25, 49, 55, 63
Boyle, P., 1
Bratlinger, E., 55
Bratz dolls, 34
Bray, C., 16, 34-36
Brindley, S., 2
Broad, E., 9, 11, 23, 43
Broad Foundation, 20-29
Broad Superintendent's Academy, 23-29
Brock, D., 18
Brown Mackie College, 39
Bunkum Award, 19, 51
Burd, S., 16, 37
bureaucracy, machine, 2
Burke, L., 19
Burns, D., 1
Burns, J., 43
Bush, J., 9-11, 50, 53-54
Bushnell, N., 43
buyback stock tactics, 16

# C
Caldas, S., 3
Callahan, D., 35, 44
Callahan, R., 58
Campbell, R., iii
Capital One Financial Corporation, 32
Career Education, 37-38
Carnegie Mellon University, 34
Carnoy, M., 9
Carr, N., 2, 49
cartels, 31
Cato Institute, 7-8
Center for Educational Reform, 7
Channel One, 12
charter schools, 21, 55
Chatterji, M., 19
cheating scandals, K-12, 42-45
Chennault, R., 51
Chiasson, A., 35
Chiefs for Change, 50
choice, 4
*Chronicle of Higher Education*, 39-41
civil privatism, 57
civil religion, public education as, 3
civil service, 57
Clark, D., 34, 46
Colchester, M., 30, 34

Colgate-Palmolive, 34
collusion, 33
commodification, 3, 11
Common Core curriculum, 10, 49
common school, ideal, 2
competitive capitalism, 3
Conason, J., 17
Condron, D., 24, 42, 47
Congress, U.S., 7
Connections Academy, 15
Consumer Financial Protection Bureau, 32
Contreras, R., 41
control, in management, 2
Cools, K., 30
Coors, J., 7
Corinthian Colleges, 37-38, 41
corporate power, 13
corruption, culture of, 37-42, 57
Costco Wholesale Corporation, 33
Council of Chief State School Officers, 49
Council on Corporate and School Partnerships, 11
Crane, P., 7
Creighton, T., iv, 62
Critchley, S., 26
Crowder, Z., 24, 26
Cuban, L., 58
Culbertson, J., iv
culture of cheating, 45-46

**D**
Davis, M., 57-58
de-construction, as discourse analysis, 26
Dell, Inc., 46
Department of Labor, U.S., 33
de-professionalization, of educational leadership, 28, 50
deVise, D., 39
DeVos Foundation (AmWay), 17
DeVry Colleges, 37
Diamondback Capital Management LLC, 35
discourse analysis, 24
Draper, W., 17
Duncan, A., 11, 23, 27, 51, 60, 62
DuVall, L., iv
Dworkin, G., 20

**E**
Eaglesham, J., 34
Economic Policy Institute, 9, 18
economics, discipline of, 5
*Economist,* 31
Edison Project, 12, 14

Edison Schools, 15
Edwards, L., 7
Education Management Corporation, 37, 40
Education Management Organization (EMO), 15, 41, 55
Ehrich, L., 79
Ekman, R., 54
El Paso, Texas, cheating scandal, 44-45
Emery, K., 6
English, F.W., 2, 20, 24-26, 53, 60
Enrich, D., 30, 34
ethic of public service, 50
Evergreen Freedom Foundation, 8
executive pay, 13

**F**
Fairclough, N., 25
fair dealing, 43
Federal Trade Commission, 31
Feith, D., 42, 44
Ferris, R., 51
Feulner, E., 7
field, concept of, 25
Field, K., 40
Fields, G., 8, 54
*Financial Times*, 30
Finland, educational reforms, 46
Finn, C., 9, 11, 20, 23, 53-54
Fitch, C., iv
Fitzpatrick, D., 31
Ford, H., 52
Forelle, C., 14
for-profit,
   free market, 2, 3
   higher education, corruption of, 37-41
   mindset, 2, 15
Foundation for Excellence and Education (Jeb Bush), 53
Friedman, M., 3-5, 11, 13, 23
   *Capitalism and Freedom*, 3-4
Friedman Foundation, 19
Friere, P., 23

**G**
Gall, M., 25
Gandhi, M., 52
Garcia, D., 20-21
Garcia, L., 44
Gardiner, S., 30
Gates, B., 11, 43
Gates Foundation, 20, 45, 49
Gee, J., 24
General Electric, 13, 34

Gerstner, L., 9, 54
George W. Bush Institute, (Dallas, Texas), 8
Georgia Bureau of Investigation, 45
Gillum, J., 44
Giroux, H., 12, 23, 63
Glass, G., 57
Glassner, B., 55
GlaxoSmithKline, 32
globalization, 12
Goldman Sachs, 16
Google, 13, 31
Gorman, P., 27
Grady, M., iv
greed, 31, 49-50, 55, 58
Green, P., 55
Greenfield, T.B., 3
Grundberg, S., 34
government, 3
Gunter, H., 1, 50

**H**
Hacker, J., 7, 47
Hall, B., 45-46
Halliday, M., 25
Hanushek, E., 9, 11
Harris, S., iv
Harvard Graduate School of Education, 23
Harvey, D., 2, 8
Heartland Institute, 8
Hechinger, J., 10
Henninger, D., 7
Heritage Action for America, 7
Heritage Foundation, 7, 19
Hernstein, R., 17
Hess, F., 10-11, 14
Hewlett-Packard, 33
Higher Education Act, 40
Hill, C., 3
Hinojosa, A., 44
Hispanics, 18
Hoffer, E., 23, 53-54
homophobia, 23
Hoover Institution, 8
Horn, C., 20
House, M., 7
Houston, P., 62
Hoyle, J., iv

**I**
ideology, concept of, 2, 54
Imagine Schools, 15

immigration, 5
immigration report (Heritage Foundation), 19
inequality, 1, 36
*iron cage*, of Max Weber, 2, 49, 52
Irvin, G., 18, 47, 55
ITT Educational Services, 37
Iyer, R., 53

**J**
Jacobs, J., 54
Jacobsen, R., 9
John M. Olin Foundation, 8
Johnson, A., 32
Johnson, W., 13
J.P. Morgan Chase, 31, 34
justice, as fairness, 36
Justice Department, U.S., 32

**K**
Katz, M., 1
Kendall, B., 33, 39
Kernan, E., 7
Kincheloe, J., 17
Kinser, K., 41
KIPP schools, 51
Klein, J., 4, 10-11, 42-43, 47-48, 57
Koch Brothers, 8
Korn, M., 40-41
Krehely, J., 7
Krippendorff, K., 55
Krugman, P., 3, 5
Kumar, R., 2
Kumashiro, K., 7-8, 24, 51

**L**
Labaree, D., 1
Ladner, M., 19
Latino immigrants, 19
Laureate Education, 37
Law, S., 35
Lawton, C., 46
Lessin, J., 12
Levine, A., 58
Libertarian Party, 8
Libor rate scandal, 34
Linebaugh, K., 12, 34
Living Legend Award, iv
Loftus, P., 32, 35
Lortie, D., 53
Lowery, L., 27
Lubienski, C., 20

Lumby, J., 79
Luskin, D., 8
Lynde and Harry Bradley Foundation, 8

**M**
Madrick, J., 3,
management, "kick ass", 42
management, by the numbers, 49
managerialism, 1, 45, 50, 53
Mann, H., 1
Manhattan Institute, 8
Maranto, R., 58
Marglin, S., 5, 31
Marrero, V., 36
Marshall, M., 33
Martin, M., iv
Martinez, B., 10
Marvel Technology Group, 34
Mattel Corporation, 34
Maxwell, L., 8, 23
McCain, J., 12
McCarthy, M., iv
McCarthy, T., 57
McGurn, W., 15, 42
McWhirter, C., 30, 45
Mead, J., 55
Messerli, J., 1
MGA Entertainment, 34
Miller, V., 23, 25, 28-29
Mintzberg, H., 2, 53
Miron, G., 9, 13, 15, 51, 55
Mishel, L., 9
misogyny, 20
Mock, V., 34
Moen, A., 34
Molnar, A., 6, 11, 17
Monahan, T., 29
money, symbol of prestige and power, 15
Monga, V., 13
monopoly, 4, 13
Moore, S., 5
Morrison, H., 27
Mullen, C., 2, 49, 60-64
Mullins, B., 42
Murdoch, R., 8, 10, 43, 47
Murray, C., 9, 17-18

**N**
Nagin, R., 30
National Education Policy Center (NEPC), 9, 15, 17, 19, 20-21, 51

National Council of Professors of Educational Administration (NCPEA), iii
National Policy Board in Educational Administration (NPBEA), iv
Needham, M., 7
Nelson, C., 9, 13, 15, 55
neoliberal, assault on public education, 3-5
neoliberal "reforms", 43
neoliberalism, 2,6, 57
  definition of, 2
neoliberal think tank research, 7
*New York Times*, 12
Newman, T., 35
Nokia Corporation, 34
Ng, S., 16

**O**

Obama administration, 51
Ohanian, S., 6
Oracle Corporation, 32
Orden, E., 30

**P**

Paige, R., 23
Panasonic Corporation, 34
Papa, R., iii-iv, 62, 79
Parsons, T., 2, 13-16
Passariello, C., 34
Pasztor, A., 33
Patrick, M., 30
Patterson, S., 31
performance pay, 16, 49
Pfizer, Inc., 35
Pickett, K., 46-47, 55
Pierson, P., 7, 47
Philadelphia school system, 18
Philips Electronic, 34
Pini, M., 15-16
Pioneer Fund, 17
PISA test scores, 10
Plitt, M., 44
Pollack, A., 33
political freedom, 3
Porter, C., 55
poverty, 47
poverty trap, 18
Powell, D., 17, 46
privatization, of public space, 13
Proctor & Gamble, 34
profit motive, 16
profitization, 14-15
Progressive Policy Institute, 20
property rights, 2

public school, definition of, 13-14
public service, concept of, 1
Public Interest, 53

**R**
racism, 18, 23
Rakoff, J., 36
Randall, M., 32
Ravitch, D., 1, 24-25, 52-53
Rawls, J., 36, 59
Reagan administration, 7
Reason Foundation, 8
reform, lexical tricks, 6
Regressionsverbot, 51
rent seeking, concept of, 31
resistance, iii, 53
*res publica*, concept of, 1
Rhee, Michelle, 8, 10-11, 44
Rice, A., 57
Richards, A., 40
Richardson, J., 51
Richwine, J., 19
Ricker, M., 32
Riley, J., 9-10, 23, 24, 51
Ritter, G., 58
Robelen, E., 55
Roosevelt, M., 27
Rothstein, J., 20
Rothstein, R., 9, 46-47
Rove, K., 10
Russell, G., iii

**S**
Saario, J., 45
Safeway, Inc., 16
Sahlberg, P., 42, 46
Saltman, K., 12, 15, 23, 26, 28
Salz, A., 30
Samier, E., 2, 49
Samsung Inc., 34
Sandel, M., 12, 36, 55
Sataline, S., 10
Saul, M., 10
Sawchuk, S., 8, 54
Scaife, Sara Mellon Foundation, 7-8
schools of education, 23
Schroeder, R., 3
Schwartz, N., 12
scientific management, 2
Scott, C., 3
Scott, R., 14

Secret, M., 33
Sinquefield, R., 10-11
Sheer, I., 33
Shireman, R., 42
Smith, J., iv
Smith, R., 25, 35
Smith Richardson Foundation, 8
social justice, 47
Sparks, S., 17
Spring, J., 55
Stager, G., 52
Starbucks, 13
state sovereignty, 8
Steinberg, S., 17
Stern, C., 46
Stiglitz, J., 18, 31, 42, 47, 55
Stout, L., 51
Strauss, V., 8
Strayer Education, Inc., 37
StudentsFirst, 8, 10
Sullivan, R., 35
Sullo, B., 44
Sun Pharmaceutical Industries, 35
superintendents, 20, 28
switchman, metaphor of, 3

**T**
Takeda Pharmaceutical Co., 35
Taylor, F., 2
Taylor, M., 16
Teach for America, 51
teacher tenure, 10
teacher unions, 11, 42, 53, 57
Teva Pharmaceutical Industries
Thomas B. Fordham Foundation, 8-9, 20, 23, 26
Thurm, S., 16
Toshiba Corporation, 34
transformational leadership, concept of, 43
transparency, 31
Trump, D., 42
Tyack, D., 1

**U**
Ujifusa, A., 50, 53
underclass, 18
United Bank of Scotland, 34
United Technologies Corporation, 33
*USA Today*, 44
U.S. Department of Education, 40
U.S. International Trade Commission, 34
U.S. Securities and Exchange Commission, 15, 38

University Council for Educational Administration (UCEA), iii
University of Phoenix, 37-38, 40

**V**
value-added analysis, 20
Vascellaro, J., 10
voluntary exchange, 4
vouchers, 4, 8, 19

**W**
Wachovia, 34
Wall-Mart Stores, 33
*Wall Street Journal,* 5, 8-9, 21, 51, 57
Walton Family Foundation, 8
Walton, J., 11
Washington, D.C. public schools, 44
Watkins, W., 1
wealth gap, 47
Weber, M., 2-4
Weinberg, N., 23-24
Weingarten, R., 58
Wells Fargo, 34
Welner, K., 17
Whalen, J., 32
White Hat Management, 15
Whittle, C., 12
Wildman, L., iv
Wilkinson, R., 46-47, 55
Wilson, R., 37
Wingfield, K., 45
Winkler, R., 38
Wolanin, T., 37
Wolcott, H., 53
Wolff, M., 8
Woods, J., 39
Woods, P., 54
Worthen, B., 32

**Y**
Yadron, D., 12
Yarmis, J., 31
Young, P., iv

**Z**
Ziebel, A., 32
Zimmerman, A., 33, 35